SCOTT FORESMAN **Reading Street**

Common
Core **101**

GRADE 4

PEARSON

Glenview, Illinois   Boston, Massachusetts   Chandler, Arizona   Upper Saddle River, New Jersey

Photographs:
Cover
Margaret M Stewart/Shutterstock

33 (R) ©lichtmeister/Fotolia

ISBN-13: 978-0-328-73366-8
ISBN-10:   0-328-73366-0

2 3 4 5 6 7 8 9 10 V011 16 15 14 13 12

Contents

Dear Teacher 5

Zoom in on Common Core 7

Content Knowledge 8

Text-Based Comprehension 10

Close Reading 12

Foundational Skills 14

Writing 16

Speaking and Listening 20

Language 22

English Language Learners (ELLs) 24

Assessment 26

Reading Street Sleuth 28

The Importance of Book Talks 32

Common Core Glossary 48

Text Complexity 55

Research into Practice 65

Love what you teach

Dear Teacher,

Welcome to the promise of the Common Core State Standards. We are excited by the opportunity to work together to make certain all children have the very best elementary literacy foundation. As your partner, we have created a tool—Common Core 101—as a place for you to find answers to the inevitable questions that this scope of change brings.

Much of what you read here is what good teachers already do. We offer some suggestions that will validate your current practices, illuminate the intention of the standards, and spark some new ways of doing things.

It is a wonderful time to be teaching. Everything we have developed for you on *Reading Street* has, at the heart of it, our hope that you will love what you teach and that your students will love what they learn.

On behalf of the Pearson family, we thank you for the work you do for children and welcome you to the exhilarating era of the Common Core.

All the best,
The Reading Street Team

PART 1

ZOOM IN ON
Common Core ©

- What do I need to know about Common Core?

- How can I be sure I am serving the Common Core State Standards?

- How will *Reading Street* help me meet the goals of the Common Core State Standards?

Content Knowledge

"No longer can we teach as we were taught. No, not in the 21st century. The Common Core State Standards speak directly to the skills and understandings all of our children and young people must master if they are to survive and thrive in the 21st century. As professional educators, we must do everything possible to ensure that all of America's young people are prepared for the future. This stands as our challenge and commitment. CCSS supports our challenge and honors our commitment."

— *Candy Dawson Boyd*

What Role Does Building Content Knowledge Play in Reading Instruction?

A key shift required by the Common Core State Standards (CCSS) is that texts must be purposefully arranged so that students develop content knowledge in science, history/social studies, and other content areas. Students can then systematically explore concepts, developing their knowledge base within and across grade levels.

By connecting what they read to concepts in science and history/social studies, students gain both general knowledge and discipline-specific expertise, thus applying literacy to understanding in other content areas (reading to learn). Informational texts also provide an ideal context for fostering the acquisition of academic vocabulary and domain-specific words.

Why Build Content Knowledge During Reading?

One benefit derived from the structure of the Common Core State Standards is a common knowledge base across all subjects—an intentional coherence of the curriculum. This coherence should increase the likelihood that students, no matter where they live, are prepared for college without the need for remediation and, further, are prepared for success in a chosen career.

In addition, many educators face rigorous state curriculum requirements in content areas. Most states require assessment of science and history/social studies content areas in addition to reading and math.

Since criterion-referenced state assessments link test questions directly to content-area standards, teachers require additional opportunities to meet standards in science and history/social studies. Therefore, structuring content-area texts at each grade level necessarily involves analyzing states' science and history/social studies standards.

How Do We Build Content Knowledge in *Reading Street*?

Students begin each day with a discussion of the concepts explored in the week's reading selections, building content knowledge during every week of instruction, across units within grades, and across grade levels. The use of high-quality informational text helps students build domain knowledge across a wide range of subject matter.

Students build oral vocabulary by acquiring academic vocabulary and domain-specific words, exemplified in each week's **Amazing Words**.

Weekly **Science and Social Studies Knowledge Goals** allow children to integrate knowledge and ideas as they access multiple texts.

A concept-related graphic organizer is developed over the course of each week, highlighting science and history/social studies words and concepts learned.

Text-Based Comprehension

"Students are expected to have many ongoing opportunities to use text to integrate knowledge and ideas, describe key details, and view text as a resource for answering questions and understanding multiple views. Adjusting your instruction to assure that text is used as the primary resource for students to meet these understandings will take you a long way toward implementing the Common Core State Standards."

— *Sharon Vaughn*

What Is Text-Based Comprehension?

The Common Core State Standards (CCSS) expect students to gather evidence, knowledge, and insight from what they read. Students build a knowledge base across a wide range of subject areas that increases with the reading of each new text.

In the classroom, a growing proportion of the curriculum is based on informational text. Discussion questions are text-dependent—in other words, answerable by looking in the text for evidence to support responses.

The following excerpt from the Grade 3 selection *Amazing Bird Nests* accompanies an example of a text-dependent and a non-text-dependent question. Remember that the CCSS expect that questions be answerable by reading the text.

"Most bird eggs hatch in about three weeks. Baby birds usually spend another couple of weeks living in the nest. Watch them and you will see how the parents feed and care for their chicks. Keep watching as your bird family grows up and, finally, flies away."

Text-dependent question About how much time passes between when a mother bird lays an egg and when the baby bird leaves the nest? (Answer found in the text)

Non-text-dependent question Where have you seen baby birds? (Students can answer without reading the text.)

Anchor Standards for Reading

The College and Career Readiness Anchor Standards for Reading call on students throughout Grades K–12 to

- determine what a text says explicitly
- interpret words and phrases as they are used in a text
- evaluate the arguments and specific claims in a text
- analyze themes or topics across texts

Why Is Text-Based Comprehension Important?

In order to attain college and career readiness, students need to have a broad knowledge base gleaned from a wide range of increasingly challenging literary and informational texts. It is important to understand the ideas as the text communicates them.

From the beginning of their reading career, students must practice the skills necessary to extract information from texts. Text-based questions can help students get in the habit of seeking vital information and retaining it.

How Does *Reading Street* Help You Guide Your Students in Text-Based Comprehension?

Teacher's Edition	**Day 1** Students read or listen to a selection and apply skills and strategies to gain meaning.
	Days 2–3 Higher-order text-based questions provide practice for students as they read the week's **main selection.**
	Day 4 Students offer text evidence in their responses to questions relating to a weekly **paired selection.**
Reading Street Sleuth	During small-group time, students read short, complex grade-level texts and apply the strategy of close reading to these selections.
Independent Reading	Independent reading provides additional practice in text-based comprehension activities that students complete on their own.

Close Reading

"Motivation is the heart of what we do as reading teachers. We know that kids become real readers when they are excited by their reading, choosing from a broad range of texts. Providing positive reading role models is a great way of showing young readers, rather than telling them, that all kinds of reading are worthwhile."

— *Jon Scieszka*

What Is Close Reading?

In order for students to gain a broader, more coherent understanding of a subject, the Common Core State Standards (CCSS) emphasize the need to read texts closely. Close reading involves focused, sustained reading and rereading of a text for the purpose of understanding key points, gathering evidence, and building knowledge. When students read closely, they give the time and attention needed to fully understand the information in a text and are able to cite specific evidence from it.

Instructional materials play an important role in close reading. Students will be motivated if the materials are of high interest and entice them to read inquisitively and carefully. Text-based discussion questions that ask students to draw evidence from the text should prompt them to use higher order thinking skills, so students analyze and evaluate what they are reading.

At times, temporary scaffolding may be needed to enable some students to read at the level required by the CCSS, but all students should experience the level of text complexity that the Common Core requires.

Anchor Standards for Reading

The College and Career Readiness Anchor Standards for Reading call on students throughout Grades K–12 to

- analyze the individuals, events, and ideas in a selection
- analyze the central ideas or themes of a text
- evaluate the arguments and specific claims in a text

Why Is Close Reading Important?

The CCSS expect the level of text complexity to increase every year of a child's schooling. As students become more adept at close reading, their knowledge about a topic grows and they are able to integrate new knowledge with previously learned ideas and concepts. This is a skill that will serve them as they progress toward college and career readiness.

How Does *Reading Street* Help You Engage Your Students in Close Reading?

Teacher's Edition	**Day 1** Teachers model the strategy of close reading. Students read or listen to the text and then apply the strategy to better understand the text.
	Days 2–3 Using the Read for Understanding Routine, students read the **main selection** multiple times. Close Reading notes guide students to use higher order thinking skills to draw more knowledge from the text.
	Day 4 Higher-order questions return students to the **paired selection** to analyze, evaluate, synthesize, and make inferences. Students cite evidence from the text.
Reading Street Sleuth	During small-group time, teachers use short, engaging, grade-level complex texts that guide close reading at students' individual levels.
Independent Reading	The suggested independent reading activities provide opportunities for students to practice close reading on their own.

Foundational Skills

"Isn't it comforting to know that the foundational skills you have emphasized in the past are the skills you should emphasize in the future? What the Common Core Foundational Skills Standards do is provide emphasis and clarity to the importance of skills that prepare students to access meaning through print."

— Deb Simmons

What Are the Common Core Foundational Skills Standards?

According to the Common Core State Standards (CCSS), the goal of the Foundational Skills standards is to foster "students' understanding and working knowledge of concepts of print, the alphabetic principle, and other basic conventions of the English writing system." How is this goal different from your goals? It probably isn't.

Before a child can learn to read and write, he or she must develop certain pre-reading skills called **concepts of print.** The CCSS expect children to demonstrate competency in concepts of print by

- knowing how to hold a book correctly
- differentiating between pictures and text
- understanding that text is read from left to right and top to bottom
- recognizing and naming all upper- and lowercase letters of the alphabet

The **alphabetic principle** is an understanding that words are made up of letters and that letters represent sounds in our language. Grasping that link is crucial as children make the vital connection between spoken and written language. The CCSS call on children to

- demonstrate knowledge of letter-sound correspondence
- decode regularly spelled words

Phonological awareness begins when a child becomes aware of individual sounds in words and is able to manipulate them. The CCSS require that children

- recognize and produce rhyming words
- blend and segment phonemes and syllables
- isolate and substitute phonemes

As children transition to learning **phonics,** and also spelling, they improve their ability to make sound-spelling correspondences. Later they gain word analysis skills, including a knowledge of prefixes and suffixes and syllabication patterns. CCSS require that children

- know and apply grade-level phonics and word analysis skills in decoding words
- identify and know the meanings of prefixes and suffixes

Text comprehension becomes possible after children are able to decode words with automaticity. The CCSS require that children read grade-appropriate text fluently and with sufficient accuracy to support comprehension.

Why Are Foundational Skills Important?

Much like the foundation of a building provides its base and support, the foundational skills of reading comprise many "building blocks" of reading—and reading cannot proceed without mastery of these skills.

How Does *Reading Street* Help You Guide Your Students to Meet the Foundational Skills Standards?

Phonemic/ Phonological Awareness	In Grades K–1, children spend part of each day identifying and discriminating between sounds of the English language.
Phonics/Word Analysis	Beginning in Grade K and continuing through Grade 3, children make a daily connection between letters and their sounds and analyze words.
Decodable Readers/Leveled Readers/eReaders	Children read decodable and leveled text to develop fluency and improve comprehension.
Fluent Reading	Children reread orally for fluency, concentrating on reading with accuracy and expression to comprehend text.
Spelling	Children use spelling patterns and generalizations to write words correctly.

Writing

"We know the best way to show young writers how to write is by providing them with powerful models of possibilities. It's essential that they study grade level models, which nudge their development to the next level. Effective writing is—as it has always been—a combination of strong content, organization, and style."

— *Jeff Anderson*

What Is the Common Core Approach to Writing?

The Common Core State Standards (CCSS) have made some important changes to the way we teach writing. But don't panic—the fundamentals are still the same. Writing instruction will continue to focus on teaching students the value of strong content, organization, and style. The goal of Common Core is to ensure college and career readiness. In order for students to achieve this, they must demonstrate command of three fundamental types of writing.

Argument/Opinion Writing

The standards expect students to write arguments in support of claims made about substantive topics or texts, using sound reasoning and relevant evidence. Arguments can be used to

- change the reader's point of view
- bring about some action or emotion on the reader's part
- to convince the reader to accept the writer's explanation or evaluation

Argumentative writing will account for 30% of the writing assignments at Grades K–5 and 35–40% at Grades 6–12.

Informative/Explanatory Writing

Students are expected to write informative/explanatory texts that investigate and explain complex ideas and information through clear organization and style. Informative/explanatory writing can be used to

- increase the reader's understanding of a subject
- explain a procedure or the steps in a process
- enhance the reader's comprehension of a concept

Informative/explanatory writing will account for 35% of the writing assignments at Grades K–5 and 35% at Grades 6–8. As students progress through the grades, they will expand their knowledge of a wide array of informative/explanatory genres and enhance their aptitude for writing in these genres.

Narrative Writing

Students will write narratives to convey real or imagined experiences, using effective storytelling techniques, vivid details, and precisely structured event sequences. Students' narrative writing will

- have a clear purpose to inform, instruct, persuade, or entertain
- provide insight into characters, using dialogue and interior monologue
- convince readers of the narrative's believability through usage of sensory details

Narrative writing will account for 35% of the writing assignments at Grades K–5 and 30% at Grades 6–8. This area of writing includes creative fictional stories, memoirs, anecdotes, and autobiographies.

What Are the Common Core Writing Skills?

There is an ever-increasing gap between the writing skills expected of high school seniors and the expectations they will have to meet after graduation. Common Core stresses the importance of progression. As students progress through the grades, their maturity as writers and knowledge of the elements of writing become more evident. The standards outline a range of skills students must demonstrate to achieve college and career readiness.

Production and Distribution of Writing

As students progress through the grades, they will learn to appreciate that a key purpose of writing is to communicate effectively to a specific audience. To achieve this, students will

- write clearly and coherently using a style and organization that are appropriate to task, purpose, and audience
- plan, revise, edit, and rewrite to develop and strengthen their writing
- publish their writing, using the Internet and other technology to interact and collaborate with others

Research to Build and Present Knowledge

While honing their writing skills, students must also develop the capacity to build knowledge on a subject in order to inform their writing. The standards will challenge students to

- enhance their understanding of a topic by conducting short research projects as well as longer ones
- integrate relevant information they have gathered from print and digital sources into their writing
- support their analysis, reflection, or research by drawing evidence from complex texts

Range of Writing

Perhaps most important of all, Common Core maintains that students must devote a substantial amount of time and effort to writing—generating numerous pieces over short and extended time frames over the course of a year. This will help students

- adapt to writing for a range of tasks, purposes, and audiences
- designate time for research, reflection, and revision
- evaluate their own writing for content, style, and organization

Why Are Writing Skills Important?

Students must learn how to create three crucial types of writing—(1) writing that offers and supports opinions, (2) writing that demonstrates understanding of a given subject, and (3) writing that conveys real and imagined experiences. Students must understand how writing is about communicating clearly to an audience, and adapting the form and content of their writing to a particular task and purpose. Being college and career ready means devoting a significant amount of time and effort to producing the kinds of quality writing expected of students after high school.

How Does *Reading Street* Help You Guide Your Students to Meet the Common Core Writing Standards?

Unit Writing Activity (Strand)	In *Reading Street,* each unit ends with a writing activity. The process is broken down into five steps—Plan and Prewrite, Draft, Revise, Edit, and Publish and Present.
Weekly Writing Activity (Strand)	Each day of instruction ends with a writing mini-lesson that helps students build on a specific writing task throughout the week.
Quick Write Routines	Routines provide students with a brief activity that may involve writing a few sentences or a paragraph and sharing it with others.
Research and Inquiry	Daily activities in the weekly Research and Inquiry project help students enhance their knowledge of subjects and inform their writing.
Reading Street Sleuth	Students hone their writing skills through the Prove-It! Sleuth Step performance task activities that emphasize expository, argumentative, and narrative writing.

Speaking and Listening

"Listening and speaking abilities develop across the years in conjunction with growth in conceptual knowledge and higher order thinking and provide the basis for understanding the content of text and expressing ideas in writing."

— *Lesley Maxwell*

What Are the Speaking and Listening Standards?

Our ways of communicating are changing, and children need sophisticated skills in order to be able to keep up with the changes. Possessing effective communication skills is an important part of the Common Core State Standards.

Oral Language Development

Studies have shown that the size of a child's vocabulary predicts his or her ability to learn to read and write. Starting in kindergarten, the standards call for children to

- participate in a range of collaborative conversations and presentations
- describe and express ideas
- ask and answer questions
- learn to follow agreed-upon rules of discussion

Higher Order Thinking and Speaking Skills

As children progress through Grades K–12, their speaking and listening tasks become more sophisticated. They begin to

- integrate and evaluate information in many formats
- respond to and build on the ideas of others
- adapt their speech to their audience and task
- demonstrate command of formal English when appropriate

Integration of Digital Media

Technology plays an expanding role in the way we communicate. The standards guide teachers as they prepare students to become enlightened consumers in the Information Age. As they progress, students are expected to

- integrate media into their oral presentations
- respond to and interpret information in diverse formats
- evaluate the credibility of information presented in diverse formats and media

Why Are Speaking and Listening Skills Important?

In order to reach the goal of College and Career Readiness, students must be effective, organized, and discriminating communicators. In college and in the workplace, speaking and listening skills are essential for acquiring and communicating knowledge and ideas, for being able to adapt speech to a variety of situations, and for evaluating others' ideas. Students must prepare to operate in the global marketplace on an equal footing with their verbally skilled peers worldwide.

How Does *Reading Street* Help You Guide Your Students to Meet the Speaking and Listening Standards?

Build Oral Language	Each day begins with a conversation designed to build oral vocabulary. **Amazing Words** help students become comfortable with general academic words and domain-specific vocabulary.
Research and Inquiry	Each week students research a topic and orally present information with supporting evidence.
Reading Street Sleuth	The Make Your Case Sleuth Step has students present their arguments and support them with evidence from the text.
Media Literacy/ Listening and Speaking	Participating in a panel discussion and leaving a voice-mail message are examples of the ways students practice speaking and listening skills each week.

Language

"The Common Core State Standards state that the inclusion of Language standards in their own strand should not be taken as an indication that the specific skills related to conventions, effective language use, and vocabulary are unimportant to reading, writing, speaking, and listening; indeed, they are inseparable. Integrative language processing means that students must understand how language functions in different contexts, make effective choices for meaning or style, and comprehend more fully when reading or listening."

— *Adria Klein*

What Are Language Skills?

We use language to communicate; it is how people understand each other. Since reading, writing, and speaking are linked together by the use of language, the Common Core State Standards (CCSS) for Language share a strong connection with the standards for Reading, Writing, and Speaking and Listening. These Language Standards are broken into the following three sections:

- Conventions of Standard English
- Knowledge of Language
- Vocabulary Acquisition and Use

Conventions of Standard English

Our language has certain rules, or conventions, which help us make our written and oral communication clear and easily understood. The standards require that students

- know and practice the conventions of grammar and mechanics
- apply the conventions of capitalization, punctuation, and spelling

Knowledge of Language

The standards for this subsection begin in Grade 2 and relate to

- understanding how language functions in different contexts
- making effective word choices for meaning or style

Vocabulary Acquisition and Use

In order to communicate successfully with others, understand complex texts, and write effectively, students need a rich and ever-expanding vocabulary. The standards call for students to

- use word analysis skills to determine word meaning
- recognize word relationships
- understand literal and figurative word meanings
- acquire and use general academic (Tier Two) and domain-specific (Tier Three) words

Why Are Language Skills Important?

Consistent language rules and knowledge of language and vocabulary promote effective communication. When everyone uses the same rules in writing and speaking, we understand each other. Not only does mastery of the conventions and functions of language pave the way for clear communication, it also creates a building block for successful writing skills.

For students who come from a variety of language backgrounds, mastery of the conventions of standard English and possession of an expanding English vocabulary allow them to communicate well in circumstances that demand a shared style of language. Such mastery makes it easier to adapt writing to the audience and purpose.

How Does *Reading Street* Help You Guide Your Students to Meet the Language Standards?

Conventions	Supported by effective, direct instruction, students complete activities to improve their understanding of English grammar and mechanics.
Selection Vocabulary	Students see, say, hear, define, and make connections with the week's selection vocabulary.
Vocabulary Skill	A weekly vocabulary skill provides tools for comprehending word meanings.

English Language Learners (ELLs)

"The Common Core State Standards (CCSS) articulate rigorous academic expectations which all students, including ELLs, are expected to attain. However, the standards recognize that ELL students are likely to require additional time to acquire both English language proficiency and content-area knowledge.

— *Jim Cummins*

How Can ELLs Meet the Expectations of the Standards?

In order to meet the criteria set forth in the standards, ELLs need to develop their oral and academic vocabularies to understand the complex language structures in content-area text to support and expand their learning.

Oral Language Development

Oral language development builds students' word consciousness and helps them develop a strong command of the English language. The standards call for students to

- participate in discussions about texts and unknown words in texts
- explore unknown and multiple-meaning words
- use language they've acquired through explicit instruction, discussion, and reading and responding to texts

Academic Vocabulary

Academic vocabulary includes content and concepts that students will encounter in the classroom and beyond. Across the grades students

- explore academic, domain-specific, and concept-related language
- use academic language to report on a topic or summarize text
- use increasingly more sophisticated academic language

Complex Text Structures

The standards require that all students comprehend increasingly complex texts that are dense with ideas and information. ELLs need guidance to understand the grammatical and linguistic structures so they can make connections among facts and ideas in these texts. Across the grades students learn to

- comprehend text structures and complex ideas within and across texts
- comprehend texts at the appropriate grade-level text complexity band
- build a broad knowledge base that will ultimately improve text comprehension

Why Are Complex Language Skills Important?

All students must understand language forms and structures that differ from ordinary social language. This is especially important for ELLs, who may need guidance and support to learn social language that will aid in the understanding of complex texts, enabling them to succeed in school and beyond.

How Does *Reading Street* Support ELLs?	
Oral Language Development	Each day begins with a discussion of the weekly concept. Students use Amazing Words to build their Tier Two and domain-specific vocabularies through guided conversations. Additional support and differentiated practice is provided in the daily small group instruction.
Academic Vocabulary Development	Vocabulary instruction is focused on language production through team talk and concept-development activities. Additional scaffolded instruction and practice is provided in small group instruction.
Understanding Complex Text Structures	Each **main** and **paired selection** has guided support so students can examine how words, phrases, sentences, and paragraphs work together in a complex text.

Assessment

"Assessment done well contributes to our effective teaching, and to our students' success. As you become familiar with the Common Core, it is important to remember that the increasingly complex performances of our students can be measured, supported and extended by quality reading assessments."

— *Peter Afflerbach*

What Is Formative Assessment? What Is Summative Assessment?

In simple terms, formative assessment can be described as assessment *for* learning and summative assessment can be described as assessment *of* learning. Both types of assessment, if used effectively, can help teachers and students gather information about learning in classrooms.

Formative assessment takes place as part of the instructional process. During formative assessment, students complete short, non-graded assignments, such as journal writing, concept maps, learning summaries, observations and discussions, or diagnostic tests and quizzes. Teachers (and sometimes students) then use the information gained to make beneficial changes in classroom instruction. Research shows that adapting instruction on the basis of evidence from formative assessments provides measurable benefits to all learners, especially low achievers.

Summative assessments, on the other hand, are often used to generate grades. Examples of summative assessments include many state assessments, chapter and unit tests, end-of-year exams, and other accountability tools. Results of summative assessments are used widely to gauge the effectiveness of curricular programs and school improvement plans, and to facilitate student placement.

How Is Assessment Changing with Common Core?

Two assessment consortia, PARCC and SMARTER Balanced, are creating digital assessments to measure student achievement. Both sets of assessments include aspects of formative and summative assessments.

- The PARCC assessment system suggests that member schools provide a formative "early assessment" – the timing of which is flexible – that acts as an early indicator of knowledge and skills, thus informing instruction. Later in the school year, PARCC's performance assessment and an end-of-year assessment are summative assessments used for accountability.
- SMARTER Balanced's assessment system allows members to administer two interim assessments early in the school year – the timing is locally determined – that may act as formative tests. During the last twelve weeks of the year, schools must give two summative tests: performance tasks and computer adaptive assessment.

What Are Performance Tasks?

Performance Tasks are an important new category of assessment in both test consortia. Performance Task items will integrate knowledge across different strands and will present students with a real-world scenario or problem. Students will have to interact with different stimuli, manage information, and plan their responses. Performance Tasks allow for multiple approaches and points of view. Research, speaking and listening, and writing are all key to effective responses on these tasks.

How Does *Reading Street* Help You Assess Your Students Effectively and Comprehensively?

Formative Assessment: Performance Tasks	*Reading Street Sleuth:* Gather Evidence, Ask Questions, Make Your Case, Prove It!
	Teacher's Edition: Monitor Progress activities; Look Back and Write
Summative Assessment: Performance Tasks	Teacher's Edition: Reading and Writing Across Texts; Research and Inquiry Project

Reading Street Sleuth

What Is *Reading Street Sleuth?*

Sleuths solve mysteries. *Reading Street Sleuth* helps readers unlock the mysteries of a text and develop ideas and opinions based on information provided in a text. It is a collection of short selections written at a higher-than-grade-level readability (based on Lexile scores) which is designed to

- meet the criterion set forth in the Common Core State Standards that students at all ability levels read complex texts
- provide engaging reading selections that promote curiosity on the part of the reader
- pose questions and assign tasks that develop thoughtful, inquisitive learners

Why Does *Reading Street Sleuth* Matter?

Research behind the Common Core State Standards shows that the difficulty of texts used in elementary classrooms has decreased over the past fifty years. As a result, Common Core has underscored the importance of building students' capacity for reading more complex texts. *Reading Street Sleuth* achieves this by

- providing a wide array of engaging selections across grade levels with increasingly challenging literary and informational content
- offering compact and focused selections that students can read and reread to carefully consider the development of ideas
- fostering rich content knowledge through independent and proficient reading and rereading of complex texts
- encouraging the development of new language and critical thinking skills that can be applied to even more complex texts

How and When Do I Use *Reading Street Sleuth?*

Reading Street Sleuth can be used independently or as part of the weekly Small Group instruction in your core reading program. Each week, students read a selection from Sleuth and explore concept words from the selection. After students read the selection, discuss questions and performance tasks that appear at the end of each selection or in the Teacher's Edition. Later in the week, students reread the selection and then they

- engage in activities or answer questions that require them to dig deeper into the text
- respond to questions that expect them to "Look for Clues" or "Gather Evidence"
- generate strong questions and build curiosity in response to the "Ask Questions" prompt
- reflect on the "Make Your Case" prompt and draw a conclusion or take a side on some issue, justifying their positions using text-based evidence

Sleuth Steps

An important goal of *Reading Street Sleuth* is to help students become thoughtful and curious readers who develop new ideas and opinions based on their reading, and who use the text to support their thinking.

To help students get there, *Reading Street Sleuth* is built around four Super Sleuth Steps that provide direction as they explore each selection. The Super Sleuth Steps provide open-ended questions that require readers to dig deeper into the text to develop new modes of thinking and new insights about a topic.

Step ❶ Look for Clues/Gather Evidence

At Grades K–2, students Look for Clues. At Grades 3–5, they Gather Evidence. In both instances, students return to the text to find clues and evidence that will help them answer the question being posed. In this step, students

- identify sequence
- look for causes and effects
- compare and contrast information
- look for bias
- determine credibility of information

Step ❷ Ask Questions

The key to understanding a text is asking rather than answering questions. Now students are asked to generate and evaluate questions based on their reading. In this step, students

- explore their interests
- think like an expert
- distinguish fact from opinion
- make connections among topics
- develop questions for inquiry

Step ③ Make Your Case

In making their case, students use the evidence they've gathered and the answers to questions they've asked to build a convincing argument. Students support their position with text evidence and prior knowledge. In this step, students

- justify what they believe and convince others
- think, debate, discuss, and think some more
- explore "layers" of thought
- draw conclusions supported with evidence
- summarize and retell key points

Step ④ Prove It!

The last step involves a performance task that gives students an opportunity to prove they've developed a deep understanding of the text and can take what they've learned to a new level. In this step, students

- prove that they've developed new insights
- make cross-curricular connections
- write, research, role-play, create art, debate
- work with partners or small groups
- have some fun with what they've learned

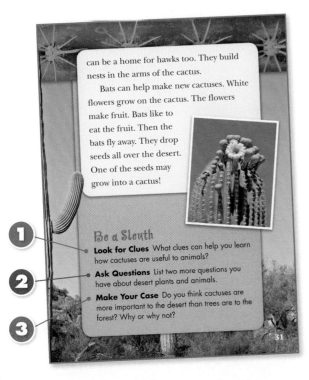

can be a home for hawks too. They build nests in the arms of the cactus.

Bats can help make new cactuses. White flowers grow on the cactus. The flowers make fruit. Bats like to eat the fruit. Then the bats fly away. They drop seeds all over the desert. One of the seeds may grow into a cactus!

Be a Sleuth

① Look for Clues What clues can help you learn how cactuses are useful to animals?

② Ask Questions List two more questions you have about desert plants and animals.

③ Make Your Case Do you think cactuses are more important to the desert than trees are to the forest? Why or why not?

31

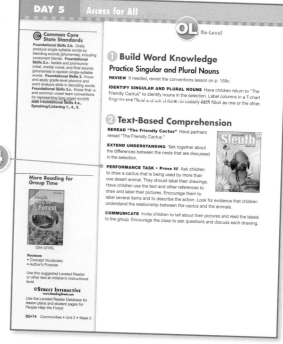

DAY 5   Access for All

OL On-Level

Common Core State Standards
Foundational Skills 2.b. Orally produce single-syllable words by blending sounds (phonemes), including consonant blends. Foundational Skills 2.c. Isolate and pronounce initial, medial vowel, and final sounds (phonemes) in spoken single-syllable words. Foundational Skills 3. Know and apply grade-level phonics and word analysis skills in decoding words. Foundational Skills 3.c. Know final -e and common vowel team conventions for representing long vowel sounds. Also Foundational Skills 4.a., Speaking/Listening 1., 4., 5.

① Build Word Knowledge
Practice Singular and Plural Nouns
REVIEW If needed, revisit the conventions lesson on p. 159c.

IDENTIFY SINGULAR AND PLURAL NOUNS Have children return to "The Friendly Cactus" to identify nouns in the selection. Label columns in a T-chart *Singular* and *Plural* and ask children to classify each noun as one or the other.

② Text-Based Comprehension
REREAD "The Friendly Cactus" Have partners reread "The Friendly Cactus."

EXTEND UNDERSTANDING Talk together about the differences between the nests that are discussed in the selection.

PERFORMANCE TASK • Prove It! Ask children to draw a cactus that is being used by more than one desert animal. They should label their drawings. Have children use the text and other references to draw and label their pictures. Encourage them to label several items and to describe the action. Look for evidence that children understand the relationship between the cactus and the animals.

COMMUNICATE Invite children to tell about their pictures and read the labels to the group. Encourage the class to ask questions and discuss each drawing.

More Reading for Group Time

ON-LEVEL

Reviews
• Concept Vocabulary
• Author's Purpose

Use this suggested Leveled Reader or other text at children's instructional level.

STREET INTERACTIVE
www.ReadingStreet.com
Use the Leveled Reader Database for lesson plans and student pages for *People Help the Forest.*

SG•74 Communities • Unit 2 • Week 5

The Importance of Book Talks

A key requirement of the Common Core State Standards for Reading is that students must be able to read texts of increasing complexity as they progress through Grades K–12.

Over the past half century, the difficulty of texts that students read in Grades K–12 has actually declined. The challenge now is to reverse that trend and help students progress on their path to college and career readiness.

How can you persuade your students to read a book in a genre not very familiar to them? How can you convince them to read more on a topic they know little about? Book talks can tempt students to read increasingly complex texts on subjects and in genres with which they are not familiar.

What Is a Book Talk?

A book talk is a kind of "teaser" or advertisement for a book, designed to convince another person that he or she will enjoy a book that you have enjoyed. You might compare a book talk to a movie trailer with exciting scenes that make you eager to see the film. Teachers and librarians can give book talks to students, and students can give book talks to other students or to teachers.

Book Talk Suggestions

Here are a few ideas to get you started.

- The purpose in giving a book talk is to make a book sound so interesting that others will want to read it.

- Students should write or carefully plan what they want to say and practice before they give the talk.

- When giving a talk on a work of fiction, it's important not to give away the ending of the book. The goal is to provide just enough information to hook the audience into wanting to read the book.

- When giving talks on works of nonfiction, asking questions can draw an audience into the subject matter. Ask questions but don't supply the answers. The audience will want to read the book to find the answers for themselves.

- Another way to grab the audience's attention is to read a short excerpt. Students should find a paragraph that provides a hint of the excitement to be found within the book.

- It's important for the person giving the talk to maintain eye contact with the audience. This helps the audience feel the excitement the speaker feels about the book.

Book Talks for Nonfiction

Spark interest in a nonfiction book by asking a series of questions that might grab others' imagination. Think about information that you found interesting or surprising in the book. Then turn that information into questions. Let's try that with the nonfiction selection *Seeing Stars* by Donna Latham. Use this technique with any type of nonfiction—expository texts, literary nonfiction, procedural texts, and even persuasive texts.

Hold the book up for students and begin by reading from the book.

"It's a perfect night for stargazing.
Twinkling stars, more than you can count,
dot the dark sky. They glow like fireflies."

Spark your audience's interest.

- Have you wondered about all the stars in the night sky?
- Have you ever wondered how far away those stars are?
- Do you think all stars are the same?
- Do we see the same stars that people saw thousands of years ago?
- If, like me, you're curious about those beautiful, twinkling points of light in the sky, read *Seeing Stars* by Donna Latham. You'll be amazed at all the star knowledge you will gain.

Book Talks for Fiction

With fiction, the story is the thing. Convince your audience that this book will have them laughing, crying, or on the edge of their seats.

Start by choosing a "hook": a paragraph or part of the story that gives an enjoyable or suspenseful preview of the book. Pique readers' interest so they think about what happens next. Use this technique with any kind of fiction.

Consider, for example, the beginning of *Because of Winn-Dixie* by Kate DiCamillo. Read a sentence or paragraph and build on it to grab students' interest.

> "My name is India Opal Buloni, and last summer my daddy, the preacher, sent me to the store for a box of macaroni-and-cheese, some white rice, and two tomatoes and I came back with a dog."

Pull your audience in.

- Have you ever been a stranger in a new place?
- Have you ever felt like you needed a good friend to listen to your problems?
- When Opal finds a dirty dog that smiles right at her in the Winn-Dixie grocery store, she knows that this dog was meant to be with her.
- If you like dogs, you will absolutely love *Because of Winn-Dixie*. Winn-Dixie is smarter, friendlier, and happier than any dog I have ever known.

Independent Reading Activities

On the following pages, we have provided several reproducible sheets for use in your Independent Stations. They include the following:

- Book talk suggestions for presenters and listeners (Post these if you like.)

- Activities for Independent Reading

- Genre worksheets for independent reading

Book Talk Presenters

1. Give book talks on books that you have read and enjoyed.

2. Know what you are going to say before you start. Write notes and then practice.

3. When giving book talks about books that are fiction, don't tell too much of the plot. Tell just enough about what happens in the book to hook the audience. Then they'll want to read the book too.

4. When giving book talks about nonfiction, ask interesting questions from the book but don't give the answers. Your audience will want to read the book to find the answers for themselves.

5. Look at your audience while you are speaking. Let them see how much you enjoyed the book.

Book Talk Listeners

1. Pay attention to the book talk. Sit quietly and listen.

2. Think about whether you would like to read the book. Does it sound exciting or interesting?

3. Be polite. Wait until the speaker has finished before asking questions or making comments.

4. If it will help you remember a question or comment you want to make, jot down a few brief notes.

5. Show the speaker that you are interested. Nod if you agree or smile if the speaker says something funny.

6. Enjoy the book talk!

Activities for Independent Reading

Book Talk Discuss with a partner your fiction and nonfiction independent reading for the week. Refer to your Reading Log and paraphrase what each section is about. Then discuss one or more of the following:

Key Ideas and Details

- List the characters in the text. How are they related to each other?

- Tell about something that happened in the text. Why did it happen?

Craft and Structure

- What happens in the beginning, middle, and end of the text?

- Why do you think the author wrote this text? List details to show why you think that.

Integration of Ideas

- Tell about the illustrations in the text. How do they help you understand events or ideas?

- Think about another story or book you have read. How is this text the same? How is it different?

Common Core State Standards

College and Career Readiness Anchor Standards for Reading 5. Analyze the structure of texts, including how specific sentences, paragraphs, and larger portions of the text (e.g., a section, chapter, scene, or stanza) relate to each other and the whole.

Name _____

Fiction

Book Title _____

Author _____

Draw 3 pictures. Show what happens in the beginning, middle, and end of the story. Label your pictures.

_____ _____ _____

- - - - - - - - - - - - - - - - - - - - - - - - - - - - - -

_____ _____ _____

© Common Core State Standards

College and Career Readiness Anchor Standards for Reading 3. Analyze how and why individuals, events, and ideas develop and interact over the course of a text.

Name _____

Nonfiction

Book Title _____

Author _____

What is this book mostly about? Draw a picture and label it.
Think about the details in the text for your labels.

```



```

_____

- -

_____

Ⓒ **Common Core State Standards**

College and Career Readiness Anchor Standards for Reading 7. Integrate and evaluate content presented in diverse media and formats, including visually and quantitatively, as well as in words.

Name _____

Genre: Expository Text

Book Title _____

Author _____

1. What is the book about?

_____

_____

2. What facts and information are in the book?

_____

_____

3. Is the book written in the present tense? How can you tell?

_____

_____

4. Are there any text features such as headings or captions in the selection? Are there charts, graphs, or photographs? How do they help you understand the text?

_____

_____

_____

Ⓒ **Common Core State Standards**

College and Career Readiness Anchor Standards for Reading 7. Integrate and evaluate content presented in diverse media and formats, including visually and quantitatively, as well as in words.

Name _____

Genre: Biography

Book Title _____

Author _____

1. Whose story does this biography tell?

_____

_____

2. Who tells this story? What is his or her view of the subject?

_____

_____

3. How are the characters, setting, and plot different from those in fiction? Use evidence from the text to support your answer.

_____

_____

4. What struggle or goal is most important in the life of the subject?

_____

_____

Ⓒ **Common Core State Standards**

College and Career Readiness Anchor Standards for Reading 1. Read closely to determine what the text says explicitly and to make logical inferences from it; cite specific textual evidence when writing or speaking to support conclusions drawn from the text.

Name _____

Genre: Fiction

Book Title _____

Author _____

1. Describe the characters and the setting.

_____

_____

_____

2. What happens in the beginning, middle, and end of the story?

_____

_____

_____

3. What problem needs to be solved? What is the resolution?

_____

_____

4. What questions did you have while reading this story?

_____

_____

ⓒ **Common Core State Standards**

College and Career Readiness Anchor Standards for Reading 1. Read closely to determine what the text says explicitly and to make logical inferences from it; cite specific textual evidence when writing or speaking to support conclusions drawn from the text.

Name _____

Genre: Expository Text

Book Title _____

Author _____

1. What is the author explaining or communicating?

_____

_____

_____

2. Is the text organized to show main idea and details? causes and effects? problem and solution? similarities and differences?

_____

3. What special vocabulary and definitions must I understand?

_____

_____

4. What graphics and text features help me understand what I am reading?

_____

_____

Ⓒ **Common Core State Standards**

College and Career Readiness Anchor Standards for Reading 4. Interpret words and phrases as they are used in a text, including determining technical, connotative, and figurative meanings, and analyze how specific word choices shape meaning or tone.

Name _____

Genre: Literary Nonfiction

Book Title _____

Author _____

1. Who or what is the subject of the book?

_____

2. Does the book have a setting, characters, a plot, and dialogue? Describe them.

_____

_____

_____

3. What do you think is the author's purpose?

_____

_____

4. What real people and events does the selection tell about?

_____

_____

_____

Ⓒ **Common Core State Standards**

College and Career Readiness Anchor Standards for Reading 3. Analyze how and why individuals, events, and ideas develop and interact over the course of a text.

Name _____

Genre: Science Fiction

Book Title _____

Author _____

1. Where does the story take place?

_____

2. Is the story happening now, long ago, or in the future?

_____

3. Describe the characters.

_____

_____

_____

4. How is the world in the story different from our actual world?

_____

_____

_____

Ⓒ **Common Core State Standards**

College and Career Readiness Anchor Standards for Reading 10. Read and comprehend complex literary and informational texts independently and proficiently.

Name _____

Genre: Realistic Fiction

Book Title _____

Author _____

1. What is the story's setting?

_____

_____

2. Does the setting seem like a real place? Why or why not? Use evidence from the text to support your answer.

_____

_____

3. What happens in the story?

_____

_____

_____

4. What events in the story could happen in real life?

_____

_____

_____

Ⓒ **Common Core State Standards**

College and Career Readiness Anchor Standards for Reading 1. Read closely to determine what the text says explicitly and to make logical inferences from it; cite specific textual evidence when writing or speaking to support conclusions drawn from the text.

Common Core **Glossary** ©

academic discussions – Engaging conversations involving targeted grade-level topics and texts that students have studied and researched in advance.

academic vocabulary – Content-area vocabulary common in complex written texts that is not normally a part of everyday speech; also known as Tier Two words.

access text – To be able to read, understand, and learn from text.

analysis – A higher order thinking skill that involves performing a careful, detailed examination of an idea or text; one of the skill levels of Bloom's Taxonomy.

anchor text – An informational text or set of texts that makes careful study worthwhile. Anchor texts provide opportunities for students to read closely and demonstrate in-depth comprehension of a specific source; they are often referred to many times and are used to link to other texts.

alphabetic principle – An understanding that words are made up of letters and that letters represent sounds in our language.

argument – A writing and speaking skill, emphasized by the Common Core State Standards (CCSS), used to develop a topic in a logical or persuasive way. Argumentative writing is distinct from persuasive writing in that it is more academic and analytical. The ability to write sound arguments is critical to college and career readiness.

close reading – Focused, sustained reading and rereading of a text for the purpose of understanding key points, gathering evidence, and building knowledge.

coherently structured curriculum – The organization of instruction so that it corresponds with the key ideas of the CCSS. The instruction should be designed to extend previous learning and maximize success in learning.

college and career readiness (CCR) – The set of knowledge and skills that students should develop within their K–12 education so that they will graduate from high school able to succeed in entry-level, credit-bearing academic college courses and in workforce training programs.

College and Career Readiness anchor standards – Broad learning expectations in specific strands (such as reading, writing, speaking and listening, and language) that are identical across all grades. The grade-specific standards correspond to the anchor standards.

Common Core State Standards (CCSS) – A set of common standards developed for the purpose of helping children in the United States receive consistent, high-quality education. The CCSS were developed by the states, and individual states have the option of adding their own standards to the CCSS.

concept-based reading – Focused reading connected to particular topics or themes that over time develop a student's knowledge base about those topics.

content knowledge – The understanding of or familiarity with a topic or discipline (e.g., history, geography, or biology). CCSS require that texts and instruction be sequenced so that, as students gain knowledge from content areas, they build a body of knowledge.

conventions – Accepted customs or practices in writing and speaking. Language conventions include the rules of grammar and usage, capitalization, punctuation, and spelling.

cross-text evaluation – A comparison and analysis across texts with regard to structure, theme, topic, and author's approach.

domain-specific vocabulary – Vocabulary specific to a particular discipline or topic, such as the human body; also known as Tier Three words.

emergent reader texts – Texts consisting of short, simple sentences that are made up of already learned high-frequency words and easily decodable words. Some emergent texts contain rebuses for words that are not yet decodable. *See also* **rebus.**

evaluation – A higher order thinking skill that involves critical thinking, analyzing what is learned from reading, and determining its merit; one of the skill levels of Bloom's Taxonomy.

evidence-based answers – Responses to questions that use information that can be readily linked to previous reading and other text sources.

exemplar texts – Sample texts that exemplify the complexity, quality, and range of genres that the CCSS require all students to engage with.

fluency – The ability to read text with accuracy, speed, and expression. Fluency is often assessed through oral reading.

focused question – A query that emphasizes a specific, precise area or topic.

formative assessment – Assessment that describes students' ongoing development and informs teacher instruction.

foundational skills – Basic skills (such as understanding concepts of print, phonological awareness, phonics, word analysis, and understanding that language is meaningful) that a child needs to master as part of the process of learning to read.

grade band – A span of grade levels used in the CCSS. For example, *Grades 9–10* is a grade band.

higher order thinking skills – The ability to evaluate, to analyze, and to synthesize information; based on the skill levels of Bloom's Taxonomy.

independent reading – Successful reading on one's own, marked by the comprehension of texts across a range of genres and disciplines.

informational text – Nonfiction, information-based texts that include literary nonfiction and historical, scientific, and technical texts. Common Core calls for an increased amount of informational texts in an elementary curriculum.

knowledge goals – Learning objectives; concepts to be mastered.

language conventionality and clarity – The degree of complexity of the language in a text; for example, whether the text is clear, literal, and contemporary or ambiguous, ironic, and archaic. Language conventionality and clarity is a qualitative measure of text complexity.

levels of meaning – The degree to which a text has levels of meaning is taken into account when considering a text's complexity. For example, texts with symbolism or satire, in which the literal meaning differs from the underlying message, may be more difficult to read than texts with an explicitly stated purpose. The levels of meaning in a text is a qualitative measure of text complexity.

literary nonfiction – A genre of text included in the range of text types that students should read during Grades K–12. Literary nonfiction includes biographies, autobiographies, essays, and speeches.

multiple sources – Two or more texts that provide information for student readers. Multiple sources may be complementary or contradictory in nature.

Partnership for Assessment of Readiness for College and Careers (PARCC) – One of two assessment consortia developing K–12 assessments to measure student achievement in relation to grade-level standards and college and career readiness. *See also* **SMARTER Balanced Assessment Consortium (SBAC)**.

performance task – An activity designed to assess children's understanding of a text or concept, in which the knowledge gained through reading is used. Performance tasks may be either formative or summative.

progressive skills – Certain language skills that are mastered at a basic level but then retaught and relearned in more advanced ways as a student's language understandings become more sophisticated. Such skills are noted with an asterisk (*) in the Common Core State Standards.

qualitative measures – Measures to assess text complexity, which include the following: levels of meaning (literary texts) or purpose (informational texts); complexity of text structure; degree of language conventionality and clarity; and knowledge demands on the reader. The qualitative measure is often arrived at through ratings of careful, accomplished readers.

quantitative measures – Measures to assess text complexity, that include the following: word length, word frequency, sentence length, and text cohesion. The quantitative measure is typically calculated by computer software.

range and quality of texts – The variety and degree of excellence expected in the selection of texts students read as they progress through Grades K–12. Exemplar texts are illustrative of the kinds of texts students should be reading. *See also* **exemplar texts.**

reader-task considerations – The use of professional judgment when deciding whether a text is appropriate for a particular student. Teachers should take into account the knowledge, interests, and abilities of a student and the task the teacher is asking that student to complete. These considerations are combined with quantitative measures and other qualitative measures of text complexity.

reader-text considerations – Characteristics of the reader (e.g., motivation, background knowledge), characteristics of the text (e.g., familiarity, level), and the way instruction is designed. These things are all taken into account when matching readers to texts.

rebus – The use of a picture in place of a word. Rebuses often replace nondecodable words in emergent reader texts.

rereading – Reading a text more than once to improve comprehension and fluency and to monitor the process of reading. Students may need to reread challenging portions of a text depending on its complexity and the task at hand. Rereading is one aspect of close reading.

scaffolding – Instructional support provided so that learners can succeed at challenging tasks. Scaffolding allows a student to complete a task or activity that he or she could not complete alone. A main purpose of scaffolding is to help students work with complex texts and tasks so that all students gain access.

SMARTER Balanced Assessment Consortium (SBAC) – One of two assessment consortia developing K–12 assessments to measure student achievement in relation to grade-level standards and college and career readiness. *See also* **Partnership for Assessment of Readiness for College and Careers (PARCC).**

structure – The organization of text information. Texts of low structural complexity tend to have simple and conventional structures, while texts of high structural complexity tend to have complicated and unconventional structures. Text structure is one of the qualitative measures of text complexity.

summative assessment – An assessment at the end of an instructional period designed to evaluate a student's competency, or progress toward benchmarks and goals, in a particular content area.

synthesis – A higher order thinking skill that involves combining information across one or more texts to create new ideas; one of the skill levels of Bloom's Taxonomy.

text-based comprehension – Understanding of a text, based on information from the text.

text-based questions – Questions that are based on information in a text rather than on a student's prior knowledge or information outside the text. The CCSS emphasize that comprehension questions should be primarily text-based.

text complexity – The degree of difficulty in reading and comprehending a text. In the CCSS, text complexity is assessed using quantitative and qualitative measures along with reader and task considerations. The CCSS expect an increase in text complexity at each grade level.

text complexity band – The measure of a text's complexity matched with a grade span. For example, in the CCSS, the Lexile ranges of 450–790 correspond to Grades 2–3.

text-dependent questions – Questions that require information or evidence from the text for answers.

text evidence – Information found in texts that can be used by students to support oral or written claims.

text sets – Related texts linked to a topic, issue, or genre specifically organized to promote the CCSS.

theme and knowledge demands – Information a student must have before reading a text in order to understand it. A text's theme and knowledge demands are considered when matching texts to students and are qualitative measures of text complexity.

using evidence – Gathering information that informs and supports writing and research projects.

writing to sources – Writing about text after close reading.

PART 2

TEXT Complexity
Common Core ©

- What is text complexity?
- How do I measure text complexity?
- What are text exemplars?

What Is Text Complexity?

Achieving Results Through the Common Core State Standards

What Is College and Career Readiness (CCR)?

A primary goal of the Common Core State Standards for Grades K–12 is to develop active, thoughtful, and engaged learners who are able to embrace the benefits and challenges of the 21st century, both in school and in the workplace. So what does this learner look like?

College- and career-ready students . . .

- Demonstrate the ability to read complex text independently
- Possess strong content knowledge
- Respond to a range of texts covering many genres and topics
- Comprehend, critique, and value evidence
- Employ technology
- Understand other cultures and perspectives

How Does Text Complexity Develop College and Career Readiness?

Defining Text Complexity

In order to become college and career ready, students need to read increasingly complex texts as they progress through Grades K–12, and they need the strategies to comprehend these texts.

The standards provide a three-part model to gauge how easy or difficult a particular text is to read. Each part of the model is of equal importance. As outlined in Appendix A of the Common Core State Standards, the three parts are:

Quantitative	Qualitative	Reader and Task
The quantitative measure is typically calculated by computer software. Quantitative measures assess word length, word frequency, sentence length, and text cohesion for a given text. These include the Dale-Chall Readability Formula, the Flesch-Kincaid Grade Level Test, and the Lexile Framework for Reading.	The qualitative measure is best addressed by an attentive human reader. Qualitative factors include levels of meaning (literary texts) or purpose (informational texts), text structure, language conventionality and clarity, and knowledge demands.	This measure focuses on the individual reader and the task or purpose for reading. A teacher is able to determine how appropriate a text may be for a specific student by considering the student's motivation, knowledge, and experience as well as the complexity of the task, and by using the teacher's professional judgment. These measures of text complexity are further developed on pages 57–59.

Reading Complex Texts

Using Text Exemplars

Appendix B of the Common Core State Standards provides lists of text exemplars (or model texts) across Grades K–12. While these texts do not represent a partial or complete reading list for any grade band, they serve the following purposes:

- Text exemplars at each grade band provide examples of the levels of complex text and the quality of texts with which all students should interact in order to achieve the goals set forth in the standards.
- Each grade band provides the breadth of texts (e.g., informational texts, literary texts, and poetry), that students should read in that particular grade band.
- The exemplar texts serve as guideposts to help educators choose texts of appropriate complexity and quality for their classrooms.

Making Sense of Complex Text

A commonly accepted measure of text difficulty is a quantitative readability score such as one that can be determined by using the Lexile, Dale-Chall, or Spache formula. These formulas are found on the Internet and involve analyzing a portion of text for average sentence length, difficulty of vocabulary, and word frequency. However, numbers arrived at by using one of these formulas should not be the sole measure by which a text is determined to be grade-level appropriate. After all, a low readability score can be heavily influenced by short sentence length without consideration of the text's subject matter or theme.

To better gauge a text's difficulty, the Common Core State Standards tell us we should also take into account certain qualitative measures and reader-task considerations when determining whether a text is appropriate for a student or group of students.

The Common Core State Standards' three-part model for measuring text complexity (pictured here) provides a balance among qualitative measures, reader-task considerations, and quantitative measures to achieve an overall text complexity recommendation. By using these three text complexity measures, teachers can support and challenge students to read more complex texts as they move toward college and career readiness.

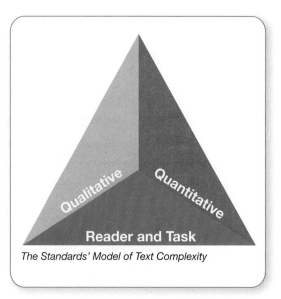

The Standards' Model of Text Complexity

So what are these quantitative and qualitative measures, and how can a teacher accurately assess text complexity? As mentioned above, in the Common Core model, quantitative measures include the computer-measured readability level or Lexile, the average sentence length in the selection, the word frequency, and, at Grade 1, the word count of a selection. Qualitative measures include a selection's levels of meaning, its structure, the degree of language conventionality and clarity, and theme and knowledge demands required of students before they read the selection. All of the selections in *Scott Foresman Reading Street* have been analyzed for text complexity. Each selection's text complexity information is available on the tab at the beginning of that week's lesson. We have included Reader and Task Suggestions to address variables specific to particular readers. In the following section we'll discuss how to determine the text complexity of other texts your students may read.

Measuring Text Complexity

The goal in increasing text reading complexity is to build reading capacity for all students. Using the Common Core model, we can measure a text's complexity by incorporating these measures:

1 Quantitative Measures

- Overall quantitative text difficulty can be determined by a readability formula. Frequently used readability formulas include Lexile, Dale-Chall, and Spache.

Grade Band	Lexile Ranges Aligned to CCR Expectations
K–1	N/A
2–3	450–790
4–5	770–980
6–8	955–1155

- Sentence length is determined by averaging the number of words in each sentence in a selection.

- Word frequency refers to how often the same words appear in a text. A low score indicates that the text most likely has words that students may not have encountered.

- The following chart, developed by Dr. Elfrieda Hiebert, shows grade-level word frequency spans and average sentence length for narrative and informational texts. These are based on an analysis of the text exemplars listed in Appendix B of the Common Core State Standards.

GRADE	2	3	4	5	6
Narrative Text					
Word Frequency	3.7–3.9	3.6–3.8	3.5–3.8	3.4–3.7	3.3–3.7
Sentence Length	8–10 words	9–11 words	10–12 words	11–13 words	12–14 words
Informational Text					
Word Frequency	3.6–3.8	3.5–3.75	3.4–3.6	3.3–3.6	3.3–3.6
Sentence Length	9–11 words	10–12 words	11–13 words	12–14 words	13–16 words

2 Qualitative Measures

Using qualitative measures to assess text complexity means making informed decisions about how difficult a text is to read. Consider the factors below when matching texts to students:

- **Levels of Meaning** Does the text have one single level of meaning (as in informational text), or does it contain hidden levels of meaning (as in the use of symbolism)? Texts with a single level of meaning are easier to comprehend.

- **Structure** How complex is the structure of the text? Is the story told in chronological order, or are there flashbacks and other manipulations of time? Is the informational text laid out in a simple format of a main idea with details and simple graphics to help convey meaning? Or is the purpose of the text not immediately obvious?

- **Language Conventionality and Clarity** Does the text contain language that is familiar, clear, and straightforward, or does it contain lots of academic language and words with multiple meanings? This will affect how easy the text is to read.

- **Theme and Knowledge Demands** How much background knowledge will a student need in order to understand the selection? Texts that don't make assumptions about a student's life experiences or familiarity with discipline-specific concepts are easier to understand.

3 Reader and Task Considerations

In addition to using quantitative and qualitative factors when deciding whether a text is appropriate for a student, it is important to consider the student's needs, interests, and abilities, and the task the student is asked to complete.

The Text Complexity Rubric in *Reading Street*

The selection *Eye of the Storm* is featured in *Scott Foresman Reading Street* as a Grade 4 title. The placement of this selection relies on many factors, as depicted in the measures in the following rubric and annotations. You can find the text-complexity information for each selection in *Reading Street* on the tab at the beginning of each lesson in the Teacher's Edition.

Use the information below and the rubric on the following page to familiarize yourself with the text complexity of *Eye of the Storm*. We have analyzed the qualitative and quantitative measures and provided Reader and Task Suggestions. Remember to alter the Reader and Task Suggestions to apply specifically to your needs.

1 Quantitative Measures

- **Lexile** The Lexile score for this selection is 1060L. That score is slightly above the text-complexity range for Grades 4–5. Students will benefit from scaffolded support.

- **Average Sentence Length:** 15.98

- **Word Frequency:** 3.52

2 Qualitative Measures

- **Levels of Meaning** Students should be able to draw conclusions about Warren's motivation to chase storms. They will need to draw meaning from a variety of formats.

- **Structure** To comprehend *Eye of the Storm,* students should be able to acquire information from a variety of formats, including charts, captions, and headings.

- **Language Conventionality and Clarity** The text uses literal, conventional language.

- **Theme and Knowledge Demands** To understand the events in *Eye of the Storm,* students should have a basic understanding of the geography of the United States.

3 Reader and Task Suggestions

Based on each student's assessment results, use the Reader and Task Suggestions from the text-complexity rubric to provide background knowledge or scaffold the selection.

Bridge to Complex Knowledge

Quantitative Measures	**Lexile**	1060L
	Average Sentence Length	15.98
	Word Frequency	3.52

Qualitative Measures	**Levels of Meaning**	understand Warren's motivation to chase storms; understand that factual information can be delivered in a variety of formats; identify realistic situations
	Structure	complex structure; chart; captions; headings
	Language Conventionality and Clarity	literal, conventional language
	Theme and Knowledge Demands	a basic knowledge of the geography of the United States

Reader-Task Suggestions

FORMATIVE ASSESSMENT Based on assessment results, use the **Reader and Task Suggestions** in Access Main Selection to scaffold the selection or support independence for students as they read *Eye of the Storm*.

READER AND TASK SUGGESTIONS	
Preparing to Read the Text	**Leveled Tasks**
<ul><li>Review skills and strategies for understanding root words.</li><li>Discuss text features an author might use to organize information.</li><li>Remind students to adjust their reading rate as they encounter challenging vocabulary and concepts.</li></ul>	<ul><li>**Theme and Knowledge Demands** If students have difficulty with the geography of the United States, have them read the selection and take notes about places to locate on a map.</li><li>**Structure** The complex structure of text on some pages may pose a problem for some readers. Point out the introductory photo caption on page 410 and the chart and pictures at the bottom of the page that provide graphic support for the text above.</li></ul>

Recommended Placement Some of the quantitative measures suggest this text might be slightly above the Grade 4–5 text-complexity band. Students will benefit from scaffolded support interpreting the more complex structure and longer sentences in this selection.

Ask the Expert
About Exemplar Texts

Dr. Elfrieda Hiebert has been involved in the development of the Common Core State Standards and has written extensively on the topics of text complexity and exemplar texts. Her work provides a wealth of information on how to improve literacy levels of beginning and struggling readers.

Appendix B of the Common Core State Standards provides lists of exemplar texts at each grade band and sample performance tasks for these texts. We asked Dr. Hiebert to discuss the role of these exemplar texts in the regular reading/language arts classroom.

What are exemplar texts, and why are they provided in the Common Core State Standards?

Text exemplars are selections of a variety of genres, including novels, stories, informational text, and poetry. At Grades K–3, read aloud stories, read aloud poetry, and read aloud informational texts are also included. These texts are considered strong examples of "the level of complexity and quality" that students need to read beginning in kindergarten and continuing through Grade 12 in order to attain college and career readiness. These texts also represent the breadth of texts that students should encounter in elementary and high school. Text selections at each grade-level band are based on complexity, quality, and range.

> "Text selections at each grade-level band are based on complexity, quality, and range."

Do the standards require a teacher to use all of the text exemplars listed for a given grade level?

The standards do not require classroom teachers to use any or all of the text exemplars listed at a given grade band. While teachers may choose texts listed in each grade-band bibliography, these texts are not meant to serve as a mandate or prescriptive for a language arts curriculum at any grade level. They are intended to serve as examples of the kinds of reading that students should encounter at each grade band. The purpose of the exemplars is to exemplify, to demonstrate, and to provide guidance for teachers as they choose texts that increase their students' capacities to read complex texts. This will enable students to develop as critical thinkers who are ready for the challenges of college and beyond.

The text of the Common Core State Standards states the following:

"The following text samples primarily serve to exemplify the level of complexity and quality that the Standards require all students in a given grade band to engage with. Additionally, they are suggestive of the breadth of texts that students should encounter in the text types required by the Standards. The choices should serve as useful guideposts in helping educators select texts of similar complexity, quality, and range for their own classrooms. They expressly do not represent a partial or complete reading list." Common Core State Standards, Appendix B, page 2

What are the performance tasks?

The performance tasks included in Appendix B provide examples of how teachers can scaffold instruction as they apply the standards using complex texts, both literary and informational. Like the text exemplars themselves, the performance tasks are intended to guide teachers as they develop new instructional strategies to meet the goals of the Common Core State Standards.

Read the following example that illustrates how the standards and the performance tasks work together to build instruction when reading *Tuck Everlasting* by Natalie Babbitt.

Common Core State Standard
Reading Literature Grade 4

3. Describe in depth a character, setting, or event in a story or drama, drawing on specific details in the text (e.g., a character's thoughts, words, or actions).

Performance Task

Students read Natalie Babbitt's *Tuck Everlasting* and describe in depth the idyllic setting of the story, drawing on specific details in the text, from the color of the sky to the sounds of the pond, to describe the scene. [RL.4.3]

Does *Scott Foresman Reading Street* provide lesson plans for the exemplar texts?

The Pearson Trade Book Library provides lesson plans for many of the selections listed on the exemplar text lists at all grade bands. Available lesson plans are located on the Pearson Leveled Reader Database.

Leveled Reader Database

PART 3

RESEARCH
into Practice
Common Core ©

- What are the research building blocks of literacy?

- What does research say about reading?

- How does *Reading Street* honor this research?

Content Knowledge
Oral Vocabulary

Text-Based Comprehension
✓ Cause and Effect
✓ Predict and Set Purpose

Fluency
Appropriate Phrasing

Selection Vocabulary

Research and Inquiry
Identify and Focus Topic

Spelling
Compound Words

Conventions
Past, Present, and Future Tenses

Handwriting
Cursive Letters aA

Writing
Formal Letter

Materials
• Student Edition
• Reader's and Writer's Notebook

Ⓒ **Bridge to Common Core**

INTEGRATION OF KNOWLEDGE/IDEAS
This week, students will read, write, and talk about weather patterns.

Texts This Week
• "Tornado Tales"
• "Name That Hurricane"
• "Hurricanes"
• *Eye of the Storm*
• "Severe Weather Safety"

Social Studies Knowledge Goals
Students will understand that
• storms affect people, animals, and other things
• storms have different qualities
• storms require preparation and safety

402j | Patterns in Nature • Unit 3 • Week 4

Street Rhymes!

Please heed my advice in severe weather:
Act quickly, find shelter, and stay together!
Get in your cellar when tornadoes strike!
In blizzards and hurricanes, stay off your bike!

• To introduce this week's concept, read aloud the poem several times and ask students to join you.

Content Knowledge 〔Zoom in on it〕

Weather Patterns

CONCEPT TALK To further explore the unit concept of Patterns in Nature, this week students will read, write, and talk about how weather patterns affect our lives. Write the Question of the Week on the board, *How do weather patterns affect our lives?*

Build Oral Language

TALK ABOUT WEATHER Have students turn to pp. 402–403 in their Student Editions. Look at each of the photos. Then use the prompts below to guide discussion and create a concept map.

• Storms are powerful weather patterns that occur in different seasons. What storms are pictured here? (snowstorms, tornadoes, hurricanes) Let's add Storms to the concept map.

• How is the blizzard affecting the man's life? (He is clearing away snow.) People clean up after a storm. Let's add *Cleanup* to the concept map.

• What are dangerous effects caused by storms? (Wind can destroy houses.) Severe storms can be dangerous. Let's add *Dangers* to the concept map.

• After discussing the photos, ask: How do weather patterns affect our lives?

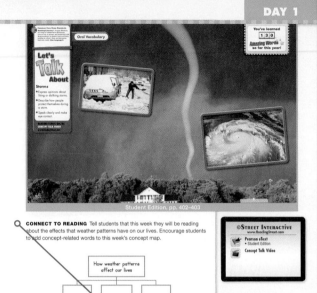

Student Edition, pp. 402–403

CONNECT TO READING Tell students that this week they will be reading about the effects that weather patterns have on our lives. Encourage students to add concept-related words to this week's concept map.

How weather patterns
affect our lives

| Storms | Cleanup | Dangers |

Ⓒ**STREET INTERACTIVE**
www.ReadingStreet.com

▸ **Pearson eText**
• Student Edition

▸ **Concept Talk Video**

ELL

Preteach Concepts Use the Day 1 instruction on ELL Poster 14 to build knowledge and oral language.
ELL Support Additional ELL support and modified instruction is provided in the *ELL Handbook* and in the ELL Support lessons found on the *Teacher Resources DVD-ROM*.

Eye of the Storm 402–403

⸺ ORAL LANGUAGE ⸺

In Reading Street

Content Knowledge To begin each day, students come together for a brief, whole-class, rich, oral language experience. Discussion of the Question of the Week guides students to activate prior knowledge and develop new knowledge and understanding of the unit concept.

Because Research Says

▸ Reading instruction builds especially on oral language. If this foundation is weak, progress in reading will be slow and uncertain. Students must have at least a basic vocabulary, a reasonable range of knowledge of the world around them, and the ability to talk about their knowledge. These abilities form the basis for comprehending text. —(Anderson, Hiebert, Scott, and Wilkinson, 1985)

⸺ ORAL LANGUAGE ⸺

In Reading Street

Deconstructing Sentences
On Days 2, 3, and 4, during Oral Language, students talk about words and sentences. They "unpack" interesting, complex sentences by breaking them up into phrasal parts. This helps draw students' attention to the parts of the sentence and the language used in each.

Because Research Says

▸ . . . the most effective method for helping students learn the language needed for text understanding . . . is through *instructional conversations* focused on language in the materials students are reading in school. . . . The conversations focus on the relationship between structure and meaning and between form and function of words, phrases, clauses, and larger segments in texts, with teachers providing students many opportunities to participate in these discussions.
—(Wong Fillmore, 2009)

⸺ ORAL LANGUAGE ⸺

In Reading Street

Connect to Reading Every week, the class creates a concept map to build comprehension of the week's concept. The map first takes shape as students explore their prior knowledge and discuss visual cues. Throughout the week, students add related concepts based on their reading and their life experiences.

Because Research Says

▸ Semantic maps address the relationships between words and concepts. Relational charts allow students to generate new information based on their reading and learning.
—(Blachowicz and Fisher, 2002)

▸ Text discussions should go beyond answering comprehension questions. Discussing text with students requires that teachers understand that meaning is not in text per se, but is to be found in the text and the experiences the reader brings to it. —(Tatum, 2005)

Common Core State Standards

Language 6. Acquire and use accurately grade-appropriate general academic and domain-specific words and phrases, including those that signal precise actions, emotions, or states of being (e.g., *quizzed, whined, stammered*) and that are basic to a particular topic (e.g., *wildlife, conservation,* and *endangered* when discussing animal preservation).

Amazing Words

You've learned **130** words so far.
You'll learn **010** words this week.

tornado   hurricane
shelter   severe
ditch   blizzard
unpredictable   meteorologists
powerful   estimate

Content Knowledge (Zoom in on)

Build Oral Vocabulary

INTRODUCE AMAZING WORDS "Tornado Tales" on p. 403b is about some strange occurrences caused by tornadoes. Tell students to listen for this week's Amazing Words—*tornado, shelter, ditch,* and *unpredictable*—as you read the Teacher Read Aloud on p. 403b.

 **Robust Vocabulary Routine**

1. **Introduce** Write the word *tornado* on the board. Have students say the word aloud with you. In "Tornado Tales," we learn that a tornado can produce some strange effects. Supply a student-friendly definition. A *tornado* is a violent, destructive windstorm in the form of a twisting funnel.

2. **Demonstrate** Have students answer questions to demonstrate understanding. What unusual effects might a tornado produce? What is the best way to stay safe during a tornado?

3. **Apply** Ask students to tell how they would react if a tornado were headed toward their community.

4. **Display the Word** Run your hand under the chunks in tor/na/do as you read it. Have students say the word again.

See p. OV•4 to teach *shelter, ditch,* and *unpredictable*.

Routines Flip Chart

AMAZING WORDS AT WORK Reread "Tornado Tales" aloud. As students listen, have them notice how the Amazing Words are used in context. To build oral vocabulary, lead the class in a discussion about the meanings of the Amazing Words.

Don't Wait Until Friday **MONITOR PROGRESS** Check Oral Vocabulary

During discussion, listen for students' use of Amazing Words.

If... students are unable to use the Amazing Words in discussion, then... use the Oral Vocabulary Routine in the Routines Flip Chart to demonstrate words in different contexts.

403a Patterns in Nature • Unit 3 • Week 4

Teacher Read Aloud

MODEL FLUENCY As you read "Tornado Tales," model appropriate expression by adjusting your voice to demonstrate a lively, fluent reader.

Tornado Tales
by Derek Elsom

The power of a tornado can produce some strange effects. Stalks of straw have been driven into a telegraph pole, planks of wood shot through a barn door, and a playing card embedded on its edge more than an inch into a wooden door. Bark has been stripped from trees and feathers plucked from chickens. The amount of feathers lost by chickens was once suggested as a way of estimating the strength of a tornado's winds.

Trains have been lifted, turned around, and dropped onto the track facing the other way. Heavy refrigerators have been carried for hundreds of yards while lighter objects have been carried for tens of miles.

A tornado passing over a pond or river can suck up the contents like a huge vacuum cleaner. Hundreds of small frogs, toads, tadpoles, fish, and weeds may be carried along for many miles until the tornado weakens and the objects fall to the ground or are flung to the side.

A nine-year-old girl living on a farm in England in 1932 suffered the strange effects of one tornado. She was out walking when a storm broke. Rain fell, but it felt soft and heavy. She shook her head and tiny frogs dropped to the ground. Her dog went berserk as frogs fell and tangled in its hair. Cows stampeded, and the terrified girl ran home to her parents. They never believed her story.

Sometimes the tornado or waterspout that causes the freak falls is seen. Often, however, eyewitnesses are left baffled. In the past these strange falls were thought to be signs that something bad would happen.

Being caught in a tornado can be very scary, but most people survive, especially if they take shelter.

In 1995, a baby boy was plucked from his cot and carried away from his destroyed home in Des Arc, Arkansas, by a tornado. He was found safe in a ditch half a mile away, muddy and with just a few scratches and bruises. In 1992, a young girl escaped unhurt after being carried almost two miles by a tornado near Shanghai, China. She was set down in a treetop.

Trying to flee from a tornado in a car is not a good idea. A tornado is too fast and the direction it travels in is too unpredictable for drivers to know where to go to avoid it. This was made clear when a tornado with 200 mph winds struck Wichita Falls, Texas, in 1979. As it approached the city, some people jumped into their cars and tried to flee the tornado by driving away from it. However, twenty-six out of the forty-three people killed and thirty out of the fifty-nine people with serious injuries were in cars. Most of the victims' homes were left undamaged by the tornado's powerful winds.

Eye of the Storm 403b

Street Interactive
www.ReadingStreet.com

Teacher Resources
• Amazing Word Cards
• ELL Support

ELL

Discuss the Read Aloud Have small groups of students discuss what they already know about tornadoes. Use the following conversation starters: How powerful is a tornado? What can the wind from a tornado move and destroy? How can you take shelter from a tornado? Share answers with the group. Use pictures from the Student Edition to provide visual support.

ELL Support for Read Aloud Use the modified Read Aloud on p. DI•94 of the ELL Support lessons on the *Teacher Resources DVD-ROM* to prepare students to listen to "Tornado Tales."

ORAL VOCABULARY

In Reading Street

Amazing Words Each week students learn a set of conceptually related Amazing Words, generally beyond their reading ability, selected from shared literature. Throughout the week students use the words in multiple contexts: in conversations about text, in retelling a story or summarizing a text, in their daily writing, and in the end-of-day discussions.

Because Research Says

A robust approach to vocabulary involves directly explaining the meanings of words along with thought-provoking, playful, and interactive follow-up.
—(Beck, McKeown, and Kucan, 2002)

FORMATIVE ASSESSMENT

In Reading Street

Monitor Progress Throughout the week, there are formative assessment opportunities in the context of classroom instruction to monitor students' progress in core areas of reading instruction such as oral vocabulary, fluency, and retelling/summarizing. Don't Wait Until Friday/Monitor Progress features provide *if..., then...* statements to help teachers evaluate the skills and respond to students' difficulties on the spot.

Because Research Says

Comprehension instruction should be accompanied by ongoing assessment. Teachers should monitor students' use of comprehension strategies and their success at understanding what they read. Results of this monitoring should, in turn, inform the teacher's instruction.
—(Duke and Pearson, 2002)

TEXT-BASED COMPREHENSION

In Reading Street

Read Aloud Each week of instruction begins with a read-aloud that supports the concept of the week, addresses the Question of the Week, and includes Amazing Words that build background for the lesson's reading selections.

Because Research Says

Teacher read-alouds can be a good starting point for introducing critical strategies for comprehension. That is, just by listening first, students can focus on the strategy being introduced without actually having to read. —(Ivey, 2002)

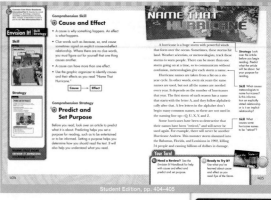

ACADEMIC VOCABULARY

In Reading Street

Academic Vocabulary During the week, the teacher directly teaches a limited number of academic vocabulary words related to reading and language arts concepts. Lessons also offer multiple strategies for developing an understanding of this academic vocabulary.

Because Research Says

When choosing words for direct instruction, include those that lead to conceptual understanding. Students need to understand these words beyond the sense of the general concept and be able to provide precision and specificity in describing the concept. The most productive direct vocabulary instruction aims at words that are of high frequency for mature language users and are found across a variety of domains. —(Beck, McKeown, and Kucan, 2002)

TEXT-BASED COMPREHENSION

In Reading Street

Comprehension Using the Student Edition lesson, the teacher instructs students in key comprehension skills and strategies using a think-aloud. Students apply the skill first through a guided practice, and then independently.

Because Research Says

Think-alouds have been shown to improve students' comprehension both when students themselves engage in the practice during reading and also when teachers routinely think aloud while reading to students. —(Duke and Pearson, 2002)

FLUENCY

In Reading Street

Model Fluent Reading As the teacher reads, he or she models one aspect of fluent reading (e.g., accuracy, appropriate rate, attending to punctuation, expression, expressing characterization). The teacher also models prosodic features such as tone of voice, use of pauses, volume, phrasing, emotion, and dialogue. After listening to the teacher model the skill, students engage in guided oral reading practice with feedback.

Because Research Says

Repeated reading practice produces significant improvement in reading speed, word recognition, and oral reading expression. Repeated reading and assisted readings may enable students to read more difficult material than they might otherwise be able to read. —(Samuels, 2002; Kuhn and Stahl, 2003; National Reading Panel, 1999)

Common Core State Standards

Writing 7. Conduct short research projects that build knowledge through investigation of different aspects of a topic. **Language 4.** Determine or clarify the meaning of unknown and multiple-meaning words and phrases based on grade 4 reading and content, choosing flexibly from a range of strategies.

Selection Vocabulary

Use the following routine to introduce this week's tested selection vocabulary.

destruction great damage; ruin

expected thought something would probably come or happen

forecasts statements of what is coming; predictions

inland in or toward the interior of a country

shatter to break into pieces

surge a swelling motion; sweep or rush, especially of waves

SEE IT/SAY IT Write *destruction*. Scan across the word with your finger as you say it: de/struc/tion.

HEAR IT Use the word in a sentence. The TV news showed the **destruction** of the building from the storm.

DEFINE IT Elicit definitions from students. How would you tell another student what *destruction* means? Clarify or give a definition when necessary. Yes, it means "knocking down" or "ruining." Restate the word in student-friendly terms. So *destruction* is extreme damage.

Team Talk Is the *destruction* caused by a tornado something to fear? Turn and talk to your partner about this. Be prepared to explain your answer. Allow students time to discuss. Ask for examples. Rephrase their examples for usage when necessary or to correct misunderstandings.

MAKE CONNECTIONS Have students discuss the word. Have you ever seen or heard of destruction? Turn and talk to your partner about it. Then be prepared to share. Have students share. Rephrase their ideas for usage when necessary or to correct misunderstandings.

RECORD Have students write the word and meaning.

Continue this routine to introduce the remaining words in this manner.

Corrective feedback If... students are having difficulty understanding, then... review the definitions in small groups.

Research and Inquiry

Step 1 Identify and Focus Topic

TEACH Discuss the Question of the Week: *How do weather patterns affect our lives?* Tell students they will research weather patterns and how they affect people's lives. They will present a report of their findings to the class on Day 5.

Think Aloud **MODEL** I'll start by making a list of topics about weather patterns and how they affect our lives. I know there are different kinds of weather patterns, so I'll narrow the topics down to one I'm interested in most. I'll choose blizzards. Some possible questions could be *How do blizzards form? Where do blizzards most often occur? What are the effects of a blizzard?*

GUIDE PRACTICE After students have chosen a topic and formulated open-ended inquiry questions, explain that tomorrow they will conduct research of their questions. Tell students that they will collect information from reference texts and online sources. To generate a research plan, help students make a list of reference texts and Web sites that they can use to gather relevant information about their research topic.

ON THEIR OWN Have students work individually, in pairs, or in small groups to write an inquiry question for their topic.

STREET INTERACTIVE
www.ReadingStreet.com

Teacher Resources
• Envision It! Pictured Vocabulary Cards
• Tested Vocabulary Cards

21st Century Skills
Internet Guy Don Leu

Weekly Inquiry Project

STEP 1	Identify and Focus Topic
STEP 2	Navigate/Search
STEP 3	Analyze Information
STEP 4	Synthesize
STEP 5	Communicate

Academic Vocabulary

A **Web site** is a place on the Internet where information about a topic is presented. Web sites used for research should be reliable and contain valid information.

ELL

Multilingual Vocabulary Students can apply knowledge of their home languages to acquire new English vocabulary by using Multilingual Vocabulary Lists (*ELL Handbook*, pp. 431–442).

ELL

If... students need more scaffolding and practice with **Vocabulary,** then... use the activities on pp. DI•92–DI•93 in the Teacher Resources section on SuccessNet.

Day 1   **SMALL GROUP TIME** • Differentiate Vocabulary, p. SG•49

OL On-Level	**SI** Strategic Intervention	**A** Advanced
• Practice Vocabulary Amazing Words	• Reteach Vocabulary Amazing Words	• Extend Vocabulary Amazing Words
• Read *Reading Street Sleuth*, pp. 38–39	• Read *Reading Street Sleuth*, pp. 38–39	• Read *Reading Street Sleuth*, pp. 38–39
		• Introduce Inquiry Project

READING VOCABULARY

In Reading Street

Selection Vocabulary The teacher introduces the lesson vocabulary words and engages students in an activity to develop word meaning.

Because Research Says

The effective vocabulary teacher presents new vocabulary in ways that model good learning. This type of instruction involves developing learners who are active, who personalize their learning, who look for multiple sources of information to build meaning, and who are playful with words. Good learners are active. As in all learning situations, having the learners actively attempting to construct their own meanings is a hallmark of good instruction. —(Blachowicz and Fisher, 2002)

21ST CENTURY SKILLS

In Reading Street

Research and Inquiry Students conduct an inquiry project connected to the weekly concept. Activities provide step-by-step instructions for formulating inquiry questions, navigating a student-friendly search engine, analyzing acquired information, synthesizing research, and communicating findings.

Because Research Says

The new literacies of the Internet include the skills necessary to successfully use and adapt to rapidly changing information and communication technologies and contexts. These skills allow us to use technology to identify important questions, locate information, critically evaluate the usefulness of that information, synthesize information to answer those questions, and then communicate the answers to others. —(Leu, Kinzer, Coiro, and Cammack, 2004)

SMALL GROUPS

In Reading Street

Small Group Time Group instruction is based on the 3-Tier Reading Model. At the start of the school year, teachers use the Baseline Group Test to make initial instructional decisions: Students with below-level performance are given Strategic Intervention instruction, those performing at grade level are placed in the On-Level group, and those who perform above grade level are given Advanced instruction.

Because Research Says

The components of effective reading instruction are the same whether the focus is prevention or intervention. By coordinating research evidence from effective classroom reading instruction with effective small-group and one-on-one reading instruction, teachers can meet the literacy needs of all students. —(Foorman and Torgesen, 2001)

Common Core State Standards
Language 1. Demonstrate command of the conventions of standard English grammar and usage when writing or speaking. **Language 2.d.** Use conventional spelling for words with common spelling patterns and for frequently occurring irregular words.

Spelling Pretest

Compound Words

INTRODUCE Compound words are words made up of two shorter words.

PRETEST Say each word, read the sentence, and repeat the word.

1. watermelon — The **watermelon** tastes sweet.
2. homemade — Max gave Mom a **homemade** gift.
3. understand — Do you **understand** the question?
4. sometimes — **Sometimes** I like to cook.
5. shoelace — Your **shoelace** is untied.
6. highway — Cars filled the busy **highway.**
7. upstairs — Go **upstairs** to the office.
8. thunderstorm — A **thunderstorm** changed our plans.
9. shortcut — Take the **shortcut** to get there quickly.
10. doorbell — I rang the **doorbell** three times.
11. jellyfish — **Jellyfish** live in the ocean.
12. touchdown — Our team won by one **touchdown.**
13. campfire — Please add wood to the **campfire.**
14. skateboard — Tom rolled down the hill on his **skateboard.**
15. anyway — It doesn't really matter **anyway.**
16. fireworks — The **fireworks** lit up the sky.
17. haircut — That child needs a **haircut.**
18. loudspeaker — She used a **loudspeaker** so she could be heard.
19. laptop — We wrote the report using our **laptop.**
20. flashlight — I used my **flashlight** to see in the dark.

Challenge words
21. masterpiece — The artist had painted her **masterpiece.**
22. stomachache — He ate too much and got a **stomachache.**
23. cliffhanger — The book had a **cliffhanger** ending.
24. sweatshirt — I wore my **sweatshirt** in gym class.
25. afterthought — She put a bow on the gift as an **afterthought.**

SELF-CORRECT Have students self-correct their pretests by rewriting misspelled words.

ON THEIR OWN Use *Let's Practice It!* p. 150 on the *Teacher Resources DVD-ROM.*

Let's Practice It! TR DVD•150

405c   Patterns in Nature • Unit 3 • Week 4

Conventions

Past, Present, and Future Tenses

MAKE CONNECTIONS To focus attention on past, present, and future tenses, call on volunteers to share something they did yesterday, something they are doing right now, and something they will do tomorrow. Students should respond in complete sentences using correct verb tenses.

TEACH Display Grammar Transparency 14, and read aloud the explanation and examples in the box. Point to the present, past, and future tense verbs.

MODEL Model by reading aloud the rest of the information in the box. Name or use the correct tense of the verbs in sentences 1 and 2.

Grammar Transparency 14, TR DVD

GUIDE PRACTICE Guide students to complete items 3–5. Remind them to check their spelling. Record the correct responses on the transparency.

APPLY Have students read sentences 6–10 on the transparency, write the verb, and circle and underline correctly.

Handwriting

MODEL LETTER FORMATION AND SMOOTHNESS Display the lowercase and capital cursive letters *a* and *A*. Follow the stroke instructions pictured to model letter formation.

Explain that writing legibly means letters are the correct size, form, and slant. The writing has smoothness—the lines are not shaky or jagged. Model writing this sentence smoothly: *Alligators live in Alabama.* Make sure the letters aren't too light, dark, or jagged.

GUIDE PRACTICE Have students write these sentences: *Anna ate apples in Arkansas. Am I Adam's friend? An ant was on Abe.* Circulate around the room, guiding students.

⊙STREET INTERACTIVE
www.ReadingStreet.com
Teacher Resources
• Let's Practice It!
• Grammar Transparency
• Daily Fix-It Transparency

⊙ Daily Fix-It
1. The thundeastorm put out our camp-fire but we had a gas stove. *(thunderstorm; campfire, but)*
2. We return Home last night soaking wet. *(returned home)*

Academic Vocabulary ⓖ
Verb tense tells when an action happens.
Present tense tells about an action that is happening now.
Past tense tells about an action that has already happened.
Future tense tells about an action that will happen in the future.

ELL
Support Grammar Have students write a sentence about what they did yesterday, what they are doing today, and what they will do tomorrow. Have students check their verbs with a partner to make sure they have the correct tenses.

Support Handwriting For students who are not accustomed to writing the capital and lowercase letters *a* and *A,* provide extra practice with place names such as Athens, Atlanta, Africa, Havana, and Alabama.

Eye of the Storm **405d**

············ LANGUAGE ARTS ············

In Reading Street

Spelling Spelling instruction begins at the sound level, moves to the structure level (word endings, prefixes, suffixes), and finally moves to the meaning level (compound words, homophones, word origins).

Because Research Says

▶ Grapheme-phoneme knowledge, also referred to as alphabetic knowledge, is essential for literacy acquisition to reach a mature state. It is important to include spelling as well as reading in this picture, because learning to read and learning to spell words in English depend on processes that are tightly interconnected. —(Ehri, 1992)

············ LANGUAGE ARTS ············

In Reading Street

Conventions Students learn a new grammar skill each week. The skill is introduced on Day 1 with the Grammar Transparency and tied to reading and writing activities throughout the week.

Because Research Says

▶ The study of grammar will help people become better users of the language, that is, more effective as listeners and speakers, and especially as readers and writers. —(Weaver, 1996)

············ LANGUAGE ARTS ············

In Reading Street

Daily Fix-It Practice sentences provide opportunities for reviewing conventions, such as spelling, grammar, and punctuation. Each sentence contains errors in previously taught skills.

Because Research Says

▶ Instead of formally teaching students grammar, we need to give them plenty of structured and unstructured opportunities to deal with language directly. —(Weaver, 1979)

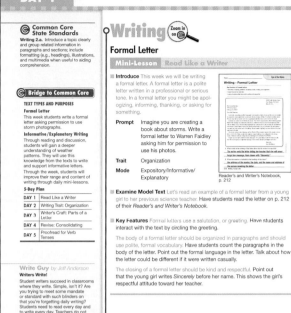

Common Core State Standards

Writing 2.a. Introduce a topic clearly and group related information in paragraphs and sections; include formatting (e.g., headings), illustrations, and multimedia when useful to aiding comprehension.

Bridge to Common Core

TEXT TYPES AND PURPOSES

Formal Letter
This week students write a formal letter asking permission to use storm photographs.

Informative/Explanatory Writing
Through reading and discussion, students will gain a deeper understanding of weather patterns. They will use this knowledge from the texts to write and support informative letters. Through the week, students will improve their range and content of writing through daily mini-lessons.

5-Day Plan

DAY 1	Read Like a Writer
DAY 2	Writing Trait: Organization
DAY 3	Writer's Craft: Parts of a Letter
DAY 4	Revise: Consolidating
DAY 5	Proofread for Verb Tenses

Write Guy by Jeff Anderson

Writers Write!
Student writers succeed in classrooms where they write. Simple, isn't it? Are you trying to meet some mandate or standard with such blinders on that you're forgetting daily writing? Students need to read every day and to write every day. Teachers do not need to read and assess everything that students write.

405e Patterns in Nature • Unit 3 • Week 4

Writing

Formal Letter

Mini-Lesson Read Like a Writer

Introduce This week we will be writing a formal letter. A formal letter is a polite letter written in a professional or serious tone. In a formal letter you might be apologizing, informing, thanking, or asking for something.

Prompt	Imagine you are creating a book about storms. Write a formal letter to Warren Faidley asking him for permission to use his photos.
Trait	Organization
Mode	Expository/Informative/Explanatory

Reader's and Writer's Notebook, p. 212

Examine Model Text Let's read an example of a formal letter from a young girl to her previous science teacher. Have students read the letter on p. 212 of their *Reader's and Writer's Notebook*.

Key Features Formal letters use a salutation, or greeting. Have students interact with the text by circling the greeting.

The body of a formal letter should be organized in paragraphs and should use polite, formal vocabulary. Have students count the paragraphs in the body of the letter. Point out the formal language in the letter. Talk about how the letter could be different if it were written casually.

The closing of a formal letter should be kind and respectful. Point out that the young girl writes *Sincerely* before her name. This shows the girl's respectful attitude toward her teacher.

Review Key Features

Review the key features of formal letters with students. You may want to post the key features in the classroom for students to refer to as they work on their formal letters.

Key Features of a Formal Letter

- Formal letters use a salutation, or greeting.
- The closing of a formal letter should be kind and respectful.
- The body of a formal letter should be organized in paragraphs and should use polite, formal vocabulary.

Routine Quick Write for Fluency Team Talk

1. **Talk** Have pairs discuss the differences between formal and informal letters.
2. **Write** Each student should write a sentence about the features of formal letter writing.
3. **Share** Partners can read one another's writing.

Routines Flip Chart

Wrap Up Your Day!

✓ **Content Knowledge** Reread "Street Rhymes!" on p. 405j to students. Ask them what they learned this week about how weather patterns affect our lives.

✓ **Oral Vocabulary** Have students use the Amazing Words they learned in context sentences.

✓ **Homework** Send home this week's Family Times newsletter on *Let's Practice It!* pp. 151–152 on the *Teacher Resources DVD-ROM*.

Let's Practice It!
TR DVD•151–152

Preview DAY 2

Tell students that tomorrow they will read about a photographer who tracks storm patterns in order to do his job.

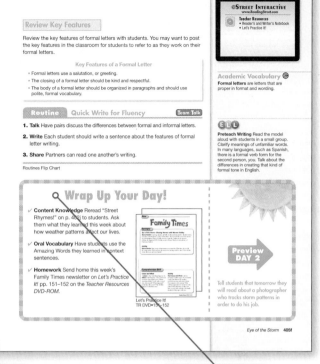

Academic Vocabulary
Formal letters are letters that are proper in format and wording.

ELL
Preteach Writing Read the model aloud with students in a small group. Clarify meanings of unfamiliar words. In many languages, such as Spanish, there is a formal verb form for the second person, *you*. Talk about the differences in creating that kind of formal tone in English.

Eye of the Storm 405f

WRITING

In Reading Street

Writing Each week, the writing lesson connects to the weekly concept and focuses on a product or form. The writing lesson begins with a genre study, which includes key features of the genre and a close study of an exemplary writing model.

Because Research Says

The writing process is a series of interactive, recursive phases, in which various stages of writing build upon one another. The phases of prewriting, drafting, sharing, revising, editing, and publishing (or making your writing public in some way) are all interdependent and overlapping, more like a scaffold in which you move to a newer, higher step all the while pulling along the best from all preceding steps. —(Spandel, 2002)

WRITING

In Reading Street

Writing Daily mini-lessons focus on the traits and the craft of writing. Following the 5–10 minute mini-lesson, students apply the trait or craft in their own writing.

Because Research Says

Learning to write should include composing staged across various phases of rumination, investigation, consultation with others, drafting, feedback, revision, and perfecting. —(National Writing Project and Nagin, 2003)

ORAL LANGUAGE

In Reading Street

Wrap Up Your Day! This end-of-the-day routine reviews the day's skill instruction, encourages discussion about shared literature and the week's concepts, and previews what's to come.

Because Research Says

For children to develop rich vocabularies, they need to have many interactions with adults. It is from these interactions that they will develop the words they need to negotiate their world. —(Stahl and Stahl, 2004)

Common Core State Standards

Foundational Skills 3.a. Use combined knowledge of all letter-sound correspondences, syllabication patterns, and morphology (e.g., roots and affixes) to read accurately unfamiliar multisyllabic words in context and out of context. **Language 4.b.** Use common, grade-appropriate Greek and Latin affixes and roots as clues to the meaning of a word (e.g., telegraph, photograph, autograph). **Language 5.** Demonstrate understanding of figurative language, word relationships, and nuances in word meanings.

Word Analysis

Latin Roots *struct, scrib, script*

TEACH Tell students that a Latin root is a word part that carries the basic meaning and comes from the Latin language. Have students identify the Latin root of each word in the chart and use it to determine the meaning of the word.

 MODEL The Latin root *struct* means "to build." Do you see the root *struct* in the word *destruction*? There is also a prefix, *de-*, which means "from, down." The suffix *-ion* makes the word a noun. Combining these word parts, I think that *destruction* means "the bringing down of a thing that was built."

Word	Root	Meaning
destruction	struct	the bringing down of something built
describe		
description		
construct		
scribble		

GUIDE PRACTICE Explain that the Latin roots *scrib* and *script* have the same meaning, "to write." Have students use the roots, together with the other word parts, to determine the meaning of each word in the chart.

ON THEIR OWN Have students use a dictionary to verify the meaning of each word. Follow the Strategy for Meaningful Word Parts to teach the word *describe*.

Routine | **Strategy for Meaningful Word Parts**

1. **Introduce Word Parts** Underline the root; circle any prefixes or suffixes. I will underline *scrib* and circle *de-*.

2. **Connect to Meaning** Define the word parts. The root *scrib* means "to write." The prefix *de-* means "down, from."

3. **Read the Word** Blend the meaningful word parts together to read *describe*. Then blend the meanings to find the meaning of *describe*. To *describe* is "to write down, or tell, what something is like."

Continue the Routine with the words *description, construct,* and *scribble.*

Routines Flip Chart

Literary Terms

Personification

TEACH Explain to students that figurative language goes beyond the literal, or everyday, meaning of words. Personification is a type of figurative language that gives nonliving objects human qualities. Personification can make writing seem more lively.

 MODEL The following sentence helps us visualize what happened during a storm: *Baseball-sized hail trampled the flowers in our garden.* The author makes the hail seem like a living thing because it tramples the flowers like a person might.

GUIDE PRACTICE Find an example of personification in *Eye of the Storm.* Be sure to point out how the text gives the qualities of a human to a nonliving thing.

ON THEIR OWN Have students look for examples of personification in other selections of their Student Edition.

Academic Vocabulary ©

personification a figure of speech that gives nonliving objects human qualities

ELL

Learning Strategies Remind students that knowing the meaning of Latin roots is a powerful strategy for learning new words. Many words are built around the Latin root *scrib,* including *scribble* and *describe.* Have students brainstorm other words that use this root. Cognate knowledge is another useful strategy for expanding vocabulary. If students are Spanish speakers, point out that the word *personification* has a Spanish cognate, *personificación.*

······ READING VOCABULARY ······

In Reading Street

Word Analysis Every week, word analysis instruction focuses on a specific skill pertaining to word structure.

Because Research Says

As part of vocabulary instruction, structural analysis of words can draw students' attention to the morphemes that compose a word, and from an analysis of the meanings of the individual morphemes, students are helped to understand the meaning of the whole word. —(Blachowicz and Fisher, 2002)

······ TEXT-BASED COMPREHENSION ······

In Reading Street

Literary Terms This instruction provides students the opportunity to analyze what they have read, focusing on text structure, literary concepts, and story elements.

Because Research Says

Comprehension improves when teachers design and implement activities that support the understanding of the texts that students will read in their classes. —(Pearson and Duke, 2002)

······ ENGLISH LANGUAGE LEARNERS ······

In Reading Street

English Language Learners English learners receive extra support to allow them to successfully participate in and progress through the daily lessons of the basic program with their peers.

Because Research Says

Given the diversity in our society, it is imperative to recognize that students may differ considerably in their inventory of skills and abilities, and these differences should not be treated as reflecting deficiencies in ability. —(Wong Filmore and Snow, 2002)

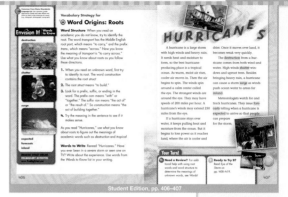

Vocabulary Skill

Root Words

READ Have students read "Hurricanes" on p. 407. Use the vocabulary skill and strategy as tools to build comprehension.

TEACH Students can use word structure to determine the meanings of English words with roots from other languages. Explain how word parts, including root words and prefixes, can help readers understand many words.

MODEL Write on the board: *Hurricanes caused destruction in the community.* Identifying the root of a word can help me figure out its meaning. The word *destruction* is derived from the Latin root *struct*, which means "to build," and the prefix *de-*, which in this case means "the opposite of." The opposite of *to build* is "to take apart or destroy." The suffix *-ion* means "the result of," so *destruction* means "the result of being destroyed." When *destruction* occurs during a storm, buildings and other things are destroyed.

GUIDE PRACTICE Write on the board: *Storm surges happen on the coast during hurricanes.* The root word *surge* is derived from an Old French word meaning "to rise, or swell with great force." Guide students in using the root to determine the meaning of the word *surges.* Have them use a dictionary or glossary to check their definitions. For additional support, use *Envision It! Pictured Vocabulary Cards* or *Tested Vocabulary Cards.*

ON THEIR OWN Have students reread "Hurricanes" on p. 407. Have them use root words, along with context clues, to define unknown words. Students can use a dictionary or glossary to look up the meanings of any selection vocabulary words they are unable to figure out. For additional practice, use *Reader's and Writer's Notebook*, p. 213.

Reader's and Writer's Notebook, p. 213

Common Core State Standards
Foundational Skills 4. Read with sufficient accuracy and fluency to support comprehension. **Foundational Skills 4.b.** Read grade-level prose and poetry orally with accuracy, appropriate rate, and expression. **Language 4.** Determine or clarify the meaning of unknown and multiple-meaning words and phrases based on grade 4 reading and content, choosing flexibly from a range of strategies. **Language 4.b.** Use common, grade-appropriate Greek and Latin affixes and roots as clues to the meaning of a word (e.g., *telegraph, photograph, autograph*).

Selection Vocabulary
destruction great damage; ruin
expected thought something would probably come or happen
forecasts statements of what is coming; predictions
inland in or toward the interior of a country
shatter to break into pieces
surge a swelling motion; sweep or rush, especially of waves

Bridge to Common Core

VOCABULARY ACQUISITION AND USE
Examining root words and word structure helps students determine the meanings of unknown words and enables them to acquire a broad range of academic and domain-specific words. By consulting a dictionary or glossary to clarify definitions, they demonstrate the ability to gather vocabulary knowledge on their own.

Vocabulary Support
Refer students to *Words!* on p. W•4 in the Student Edition for additional practice.

406e Patterns in Nature • Unit 3 • Week 4

Vocabulary Strategy for
Word Origins: Roots

Word Structure When you read an academic you do not know, try to identify the root. The word *transport* has the Middle English root *port*, which means "across," and the prefix *trans-*, which means "across." Now you know the meaning of *transport* is "to carry across." Use what you know about roots as you follow these directions.

1. When you read an unknown word, first try to identify its root. The word construction contains the root *struct*

2. The root *struct* means "to build."

3. Look for a prefix, suffix, or ending in the word. The prefix *con-* means "with" or "together." The suffix *-ion* means "the act of" or "the result of." So *construction* means "the act of building together."

4. Try the meaning in the sentence to see if it makes sense.

As you read "Hurricanes," use what you know about roots to figure out the meanings of academic words such as *destruction* and *tropical*

Words to Write Reread "Hurricanes." Have you ever been in a severe storm or seen one on TV? Write about the experience. Use words from the *Words to Know* list in your writing.

Your Turn!

Need a Review? For additional help with using root words and word structure to determine the meanings of unknown words, see *Words!*

Ready to Try It? Read *Eye of the Storm* on pp. 408-419.

Student Edition, pp. 406-407

HURRICANES

A hurricane is a large storm with high winds and heavy rain. It needs heat and moisture to form, so the best hurricane-producing place is a tropical ocean. As warm, moist air rises, cooler air moves in. Then the air begins to spin. The winds spin around a calm center called the eye. The strongest winds are around the eye. They may have speeds of 200 miles per hour. A hurricane's winds may extend 250 miles from the eye.

If a hurricane stays over water, it keeps pulling heat and moisture from the ocean. But it begins to lose power as it reaches land, where the air is cooler and

drier. Once it moves over land, it becomes weak very quickly.

The *destruction* from a hurricane comes from both wind and water. High winds shatter windows and uproot trees. Besides bringing heavy rain, a hurricane can cause a storm *surge* or winds push ocean water to areas far inland.

Meteorologists watch for and track hurricanes. They issue forecasts telling when a hurricane is expected to arrive so that people can prepare for the storm.

406 • 407

Reread for Fluency

APPROPRIATE PHRASING Read paragraph one of "Hurricanes," keeping your pace slow and steady. Tell students that punctuation cues such as periods and commas show you where to pause and help you read words in meaningful phrases that your listeners will easily understand.

Routine Oral Rereading

1. **Read** Have students read paragraph one of "Hurricanes" orally.

2. **Reread** To achieve optimal fluency, students should reread the text three or four times.

3. **Corrective Feedback** Have students read aloud without you. Provide feedback about the way they group words together and encourage them to pay careful attention to punctuation cues. Listen for use of appropriate phrasing.

Routines Flip Chart

STREET INTERACTIVE
www.ReadingStreet.com

Pearson eText
• Student Edition

Vocabulary Activities

Journal

Teacher Resources
• Envision It! Pictured Vocabulary Cards
• Tested Vocabulary Cards
• Reader's and Writer's Notebook

Eye of the Storm 406-407

In Reading Street

Vocabulary Skill Students' word knowledge is expanded by introducing them to word-learning strategies and skills. Using words from the selection, the teacher explains the skill. Then students provide additional examples.

Because Research Says

Effective vocabulary teaching in the early years should make students curious about words. To be a good word learner, one must be hungry for words. Learning (and using) new words can be exciting because a new word not only is a sign of growing up but it also is a sign of greater control and under-standing about one's world.
—(Stahl and Stahl, 2004)

Text-Based Comprehension

Introduce Main Selection

Zoom in on

Student Edition, pp. 408–409

GENRE Remind students that **expository text** tells about real people, places, and events. Expository texts often use text features such as heads and subheads to organize information. Features such as guide words, photos, and captions are included to help readers better understand the text.

PREVIEW AND PREDICT Have students preview the title, photographs, and captions in *Eye of the Storm*. Ask students to predict what they will find out as they read.

PURPOSE By analyzing *Eye of the Storm*, an expository text, students will gain knowledge of weather patterns.

408–409 Patterns in Nature • Unit 3 • Week 4

Common Core State Standards

Informational Text 3. Explain events, procedures, ideas, or concepts in a historical, scientific, or technical text, including what happened and why, based on specific information in the text. **Informational Text 10.** By the end of year, read and comprehend informational texts, including history/social studies, science, and technical texts, in the grades 4–5 text complexity band proficiently, with scaffolding as needed at the high end of the range.

Bridge to Common Core

CRAFT AND STRUCTURE

Students analyze the structure of the selection and how its components relate to each other and the whole when they examine its genre. As they preview the selection and prepare to read, they come to see how purpose drives the content and style of the text.

Academic Vocabulary

expository text informational writing that explains an object, idea, or theme

Strategy Response Log

Have students use p. 20 in the *Reader's and Writer's Notebook* to set a purpose for reading and to make predictions about *Eye of the Storm*.

Access Main Selection

READER AND TASK SUGGESTIONS	
Preparing to Read the Text	**Leveled Tasks**
• Review skills and strategies for understanding root words. • Discuss text features an author might use to organize information. • Remind students to adjust their reading rate as they encounter challenging vocabulary and concepts.	• **Theme and Knowledge Demands** If students have difficulty with U.S. geography, have them read the selection and take notes about places to locate on a map. • **Structure** The complex structure of text on some pages may pose a problem for some readers. Point out that there is an introductory photo caption, followed by text from the story. The chart and pictures at the bottom of the page provide graphic support for the text above.

See Text Complexity Measures for *Eye of the Storm* on the tab at the beginning of this week.

READ Tell students that today they will read *Eye of the Storm* for the first time. Use the Read for Understanding routine.

Routine   Read for Understanding

Deepen understanding by reading the selection multiple times.

1. **First Read**—If students need help, use the **Access Text** note to help them clarify understanding.

2. **Second Read**—Use the **Close Reading** notes to help students draw knowledge from the text.

Day 2   SMALL GROUP TIME • Differentiate Comprehension, p. SG•49

OL On-Level	SI Strategic Intervention	A Advanced
• **Practice** Selection Vocabulary • **Read** *Eye of the Storm*	• **Reteach** Selection Vocabulary • **Read** *Eye of the Storm*	• **Extend** Selection Vocabulary • **Read** *Eye of the Storm* • **Investigate** Inquiry Project

Eye of the Storm **409a**

Street Interactive
www.ReadingStreet.com

Pearson eText
• Student Edition

Teacher Resources
• Reader's and Writer's Notebook
• AudioText CD
• Background Building Audio CD

Access for All

SI Strategic Intervention
Work with students to set a purpose for reading, or if time permits, have students work with partners to set purposes.

A Advanced
Have students find out how many hurricanes the East and Gulf coasts of the United States had during the last hurricane season.

ELL
Build Background To build background, review the selection summary in English (*ELL Handbook* p. 109). Use the Retelling Cards to provide visual support for the summary.

ELL
If... students need more scaffolding and practice with the **Comprehension Skill,** **then...** use the activities on p. DI•96 in the Teacher Resources section on SuccessNet.

TEXT-BASED COMPREHENSION

In Reading Street

Text Complexity Each week there are Reader and Task Suggestions for helping students access the varied, complex texts they will encounter. In addition, text complexity measures for each selection can be found on the weekly tabs.

Because Research Says

▸ . . . effective and engaged comprehenders tend to read more than their struggling counterparts. Particularly, the volume of experiences students have interacting with texts both in and out of the classroom significantly correlates with their overall reading success. —(Duke, Pearson, Strachan, and Billman, 2011)

▸ Instruction that includes hands-on activities, opportunities to engage in reading for authentic purposes, and texts with a clear structure and vivid, concrete examples is associated with motivated engagement and, subsequently, better recall and learning. —(Duke, Pearson, Strachan, and Billman, 2011)

TEXT-BASED COMPREHENSION

In Reading Street

Read for Understanding Routine Students read the weekly selection multiple times for different purposes. This process of reading and rereading helps students access complex texts and gain deeper knowledge from what they read.

Because Research Says

▸ We bring knowledge to the comprehension process, and that knowledge shapes our comprehension. When we comprehend, we gain new information that changes our knowledge, which is then available for later comprehension. So, in that positive, virtuous cycle, knowledge begets comprehension, which begets knowledge, and so on. In a very real sense, we literally read and learn our way into greater knowledge about the world and greater comprehension capacity. —(Duke, Pearson, Strachan, and Billman, 2011)

SMALL GROUPS

In Reading Street

Access for All: Strategic Intervention Students who are struggling receive more explicit, intensive instruction, more scaffolding, more practice with critical skills, and more opportunities to respond.

Because Research Says

▸ A consistent finding in meta-analyses examining effective instructional practices for students with reading and learning disabilities is that a combination of explicit and systematic instruction that provides modeling and feedback is associated with improved academic outcomes. —(Vaughn and Linan-Thompson, 2003)

1ST READ

Access Text ⓒ If students need help, then...

ⓦ PREDICT AND SET PURPOSE Have students read paragraph 1 on p. 412 and look at the pictures. Have them use this information to predict what the rest of this section will be about and to set a purpose for reading.

MODEL The photos show stormy weather, and I see Warren sitting in his SUV studying a map. The text tells me that he looks at satellite pictures and listens to forecasters when a hurricane is forming. I predict Warren will travel to an area where a hurricane is going to hit. I'll read on to find out what he does next.

ON THEIR OWN Have students finish reading p. 412 to confirm their predictions and to predict what Warren will do once he gets to the East Coast.

DEVELOP LANGUAGE Have students reread the first paragraph on p. 413. What does *destruction* mean? What are some examples of destruction that might be caused by hurricanes?

"Shadow Chaser is Warren's specially equipped four-wheel-drive vehicle."

412

Student Edition, p. 412

413

Student Edition, p. 413

2ND READ

Close Reading ⓒ

ANALYSIS • TEXT EVIDENCE Reread pages 412–413 to find two effects of hurricanes. Cite evidence from the text to support your response. (One effect on p. 412 is that branches and boards can shatter windows and damage cars. A second effect on p. 413 is that powerful winds can lift the seawater and carry it inland as a storm surge.)

EVALUATION • TEXT EVIDENCE Do you think Warren prefers to photograph tornadoes or hurricanes? Why? (I think Warren would rather take pictures of a hurricane because it is too dangerous to photograph a tornado as it happens.)

412–413　Patterns in Nature • Unit 3 • Week 4

Eye of the Storm　413a

ⓒ **Common Core State Standards**
Informational Text 1. Refer to details and examples in a text when explaining what the text says explicitly and when drawing inferences from the text. **Also Informational Text 5.**

Connect to Social Studies
Storm Surge Serious damage from hurricanes often results from storm surge flooding. A storm surge occurs when the winds of a tropical storm push the water over the land along the coast. In addition to flooding, a storm surge can cause a widespread loss of land along the shoreline.

ELL
Extend Language Invite students to compare key storm-related terms such as *hurricane, tornado, satellite,* and *meteorologists* to equivalent terms in their first language. If students are Spanish speakers, point out Spanish cognates *huracán* (hurricane), *tornado* (tornado), *satélite* (satellite), and *meteorólogo* (meteorologist).

TEXT-BASED COMPREHENSION

In Reading Street

Access Text During the first read of the selection, students respond to questions that address a skill or strategy in context. If students have difficulty answering a question, the teacher models a response and then guides students through a quick activity in which students' ability to apply the skill or strategy is assessed.

Because Research Says

Good comprehenders have learned that they have control of the reading process. They actively construct meaning as they read by directing their own comprehension using basic strategies. They know reading works because they have knowledge about how sounds, letters, and print work; they know what strategies to use to help them understand; and they know when to use which strategies. —(Blachowicz and Ogle, 2001)

TEXT-BASED COMPREHENSION

In Reading Street

Close Reading During the second read of the selection, students draw knowledge from the text and respond to questions that require using the higher-order thinking skills of analysis, synthesis, and evaluation. Students often cite evidence from the text to support their responses.

Because Research Says

Most effective teachers engage children in more higher-level responses to text (both in discussions and written assignments) as part of what the researchers labeled a framework of instruction promoting cognitive engagement during reading. —(Taylor, Pearson, Peterson, and Rodriguez, 2005)

INFORMATIONAL TEXT

In Reading Street

Connect to Social Studies Instruction is organized around unit themes that emphasize science and social studies concepts. As students read the selections, they have multiple opportunities to make connections to science and social studies concepts.

Because Research Says

When concept goals were prominent in reading, students focused on gaining meaning, building knowledge, and understanding deeply. Meaningful conceptual content in reading instruction increases motivation for reading and text comprehension. —(Guthrie, et al., 2004)

Common Core State Standards

Writing 2.a. Introduce a topic clearly and group related information in paragraphs and sections; include formatting (e.g., headings), illustrations, and multimedia when useful to aiding comprehension. **Writing 4.** Produce clear and coherent writing in which the development and organization are appropriate to task, purpose, and audience.

Writing （Zoom in on）

Formal Letter

[Writing Trait: Organization]

INTRODUCE THE PROMPT Remind students that the selection they are reading this week, *Eye of the Storm*, is an example of an expository text. Tell students that they will be writing a formal letter to the author of the expository text. Remind them that they should think about the features of a formal letter as they plan their writing. Read aloud the writing prompt.

Writing Prompt

Imagine you are creating a book about storms. Write a formal letter to Warren Faidley asking him for permission to use his photos.

（Think Aloud）**SELECT A TOPIC** To help choose what we will write in our letter, let's make a chart and list ideas that might help us know what to write. **Display a T-chart.** In *Eye of the Storm*, you saw some incredible photos and learned about the photographer who takes those pictures. Let's start the T-chart explaining why you liked the photos and the photographer who took them.

GATHER INFORMATION Remind students that they can do research to help them find more information about Warren Faidley. Remember to keep this chart, as students will refer back to it tomorrow as they draft.

What I like about Warren Faidley	What I like about Warren Faidley's photography
He is adventurous.	The images seem to come alive.
He has an interesting perspective— seeing storms from the inside out.	The photos seem extremely clear for being in the middle of a storm.
He is a talented photographer.	The photos are rare because not many people stay in the middle of a storm.

Corrective feedback	Circulate around the room, assisting students with their charts. When they're finished, direct students to pick out a few things that they would like to use in their letter to Warren Faidley. If students are having trouble, allow them to brainstorm with partners, using the chart on the board as a starting point.

[Mini-Lesson]　Writing Trait: Organization

■ When writing a formal letter, it's important to organize your thoughts. **Display an outline.** You need to figure out what you want to say in the body of the letter. In this letter, we are going to ask Warren Faidley for something. First, we should start by introducing ourselves. Write *Introduction* on line A. On the lines underneath, explain that you will write a few sentences telling Mr. Faidley who you are. On line B, write *What I like about Mr. Faidley and his photographs.* In this section, I will write about what I like about Mr. Faidley's photos.

■ Transfer the best ideas from the T-chart onto the lines below line B. This information will help me as I write my body paragraphs. On line C, I'll write my request. Have students begin their own outline using the form on p. 216 of their *Reader's and Writer's Notebook*.

[Routine]　Quick Write for Fluency　[Team Talk]

1. Talk Have pairs discuss what they like about Warren Faidley.

2. Write Each student writes two sentences about Mr. Faidley.

3. Share Partners read their sentences to each other.

Routines Flip Chart

STREET INTERACTIVE
www.ReadingStreet.com
Teacher Resources
• Reader's and Writer's Notebook
• Graphic Organizer

| Outline Form A |
| Title |
| A. |
| B. |
| C. |

Reader's and Writer's Notebook, p. 216

Wrap Up Your Day!

✓ **Content Knowledge** Have students discuss how weather patterns affect Warren Faidley's job.

✓ **Text-Based Comprehension** What happens when the Atlantic Ocean warms up in the late summer and early fall?

Preview DAY 3

Tell students that tomorrow they will read more about a photographer who tracks storms.

····· WRITING ·····

In Reading Street

Writing Traits Teachers are provided with prompts that focus on the week's concept, oral vocabulary, grammar lesson, and featured writing trait.

Because Research Says

▶ Learning to write should include composing staged across various phases of rumination, investigation, consultation with others, drafting, feedback, revision, and perfecting. —(National Writing Project and Nagin, 2003)

····· WRITING ·····

In Reading Street

Quick Write for Fluency Students engage in daily writing activities to develop language, grammar, and writing skills. The routine focuses on the development of writing fluency.

Because Research Says

▶ Writing has to be learned in school very much the same way that it is practiced out of school. This means that the writer has a reason to write, an intended audience, and control of subject and form. —(National Writing Project and Nagin, 2003)

Common Core State Standards
Informational Text 1. Refer to details and examples in a text when explaining what the text says explicitly and when drawing inferences from the text. **Informational Text 2.** Determine the main idea of a text and explain how it is supported by key details; summarize the text.

Strategy Response Log
Have students revise their predictions and set a new purpose for reading on p. 20 in the *Reader's and Writer's Notebook*.

Text-Based Comprehension

Zoom in on

Check Understanding

Student Edition, pp. 408–409

If... you chose to read *Eye of the Storm* in two parts,
then... use the following questions to monitor students' understanding of pp. 408–415 of the selection. Encourage students to cite evidence from the text.

INFERENCE What causes Warren to fly to cities near the place where a hurricane is expected? (Flying is faster than driving, and a car can be destroyed during a hurricane.) (p. 412)

SYNTHESIS Why do you think the command center held stockpiles of necessary supplies? (The extra food and water were there in case the men could not get supplies for several days. The rope was there to tie things down or help them in emergency situations.) (p. 415)

RETELL Have students retell the "Chasing Hurricanes" section, pp. 411–413, from *Eye of the Storm*, referring to details in the text. Encourage students to use the text features in their retellings.

READ Use the **Access Text** and **Close Reading** notes to finish reading *Eye of the Storm*.

| Corrective feedback | **If...** students leave out important details, **then...** have students look back through the photographs in the selection. |

416c Patterns in Nature • Unit 3 • Week 4

If... you followed the Read for Understanding routine below,
then... ask students to retell the selection before you reread *Eye of the Storm*.

RETELL Have students retell the "Chasing Hurricanes" section, pp. 411–413, from *Eye of the Storm*, referring to details in the text. Encourage students to use the text features in their retellings.

| Corrective feedback | **If...** students leave out important details, **then...** have students look back through the photographs in the selection. |

READ Return to p. 410–411 and use the **2nd Read/Close Reading** notes to reread *Eye of the Storm*.

Read Main Selection

Routine **Read for Understanding**

Deepen understanding by reading the selection multiple times.

1. **First Read**—If students need help, use the **Access Text** note to help them clarify understanding.

2. **Second Read**—Use the **Close Reading** notes to help students draw knowledge from the text.

eStreet Interactive
www.ReadingStreet.com

Pearson eText
• Student Edition

Teacher Resources
• Reader's and Writer's Notebook
• AudioText CD

ELL
Check Retelling To support retelling, review the multilingual summary for *Eye of the Storm* with the appropriate Retelling Cards to scaffold understanding.

ELL
If... students need more scaffolding and practice with the **Main Selection,**
then... use the activities on p. DI•97 in the Teacher Resources section on SuccessNet.

Day 3 **SMALL GROUP TIME** • Differentiate Close Reading, p. SG•49

OL On-Level	**SI Strategic Intervention**	**A Advanced**
• **Reread** to Develop Vocabulary	• **Reread** to Develop Vocabulary	• **Reread** to Extend Vocabulary
• **Read** *Eye of the Storm*	• **Read** *Eye of the Storm*	• **Read** *Eye of the Storm*
		• **Investigate** Inquiry Project

Eye of the Storm 416d

TEXT-BASED COMPREHENSION

In Reading Street

Strategy Response Log
Students keep a Strategy Response Log to record their use of a specific strategy and do a mid-selection self-check on their use of the strategy. The teacher monitors their progress on how and when they apply the strategy and coaches them as necessary. After reading, students look back on how and when they applied the strategy. Students then apply it to their independent reading.

Because Research Says
Comprehension processes instruction is about encouraging young readers to be cognitively active as they read, just the way that mature, excellent readers are active cognitively. —(Block and Pressley, 2003)

TEXT-BASED COMPREHENSION

In Reading Street

Check Understanding
Text-based comprehension questions provide opportunities for discussion and skill application. Students retell what they have read and answer questions that require analysis, synthesis, inference, or evaluation.

Because Research Says
The model of comprehension instruction best supported by research has five components: (1) an explicit description of the strategy/skill and when and how it should be used; (2) teacher modeling the strategy/skill in action, usually by thinking aloud; (3) collaborative use of the strategy/skill in action; (4) guided practice using the strategy/skill with gradual release of responsibility; and (5) independent use of the strategy/skill. —(Duke and Pearson, 2002)

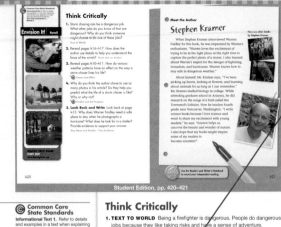

WRITING

In Reading Street

Look Back and Write Students respond to a question that sends them back into the selection and then write their response, focusing on the skill, strategy, or both. A scoring rubric serves as an assessment tool for the teacher.

Because Research Says

Writing is a more complex activity; more than just a skill or talent, it is a means in inquiry and expression for learning in all grades and disciplines.
—(National Writing Project and Nagin, 2003)

TEXT-BASED COMPREHENSION

In Reading Street

Retell With the assistance of the retelling strip in the Student Edition or the Story Sort online, students retell narrative text or summarize expository text. A scoring rubric serves as an assessment tool for the teacher.

Because Research Says

Oral retelling provides information as a process and a product. It allows teachers to assess what students remember about what they read without direct questioning or support from a teacher. —(Paratore and McCormack, 2005)

Practice, guidance, and evaluation of stories retold and rewritten have been found to improve children's written and oral original stories.
—(Morrow, 1996)

Common Core State Standards

Informational Text 7. Interpret information presented visually, orally, or quantitatively (e.g., in charts, graphs, diagrams, time lines, animations, or interactive elements on Web pages) and explain how the information contributes to an understanding of the text in which it appears. **Foundational Skills 4.** Read with sufficient accuracy and fluency to support comprehension. **Foundational Skills 4.b.** Read grade-level prose and poetry orally with accuracy, appropriate rate, and expression. **Foundational Skills 4.c.** Use context to confirm or self-correct word recognition and understanding, rereading as necessary.

Fluency

Appropriate Phrasing

MODEL FLUENT READING Have students turn to p. 412 of *Eye of the Storm.* Have students follow along as you read the page. Tell them to listen to the way you use punctuation cues to group words in meaningful phrases as you read with fluency about Warren Faidley tracking hurricanes to photograph.

GUIDE PRACTICE Have students follow along as you read the page again. Ask questions to be sure they comprehend the text. Then have them reread the page as a group without you until they read with no mistakes, using punctuation cues to achieve appropriate phrasing. Continue in the same way on p. 413.

Corrective feedback	**If...** students are having difficulty reading with correct phrasing, **then...** prompt them as follows: • Where can we break up this sentence? Which words are related? • Read the sentence again. Pause after each group of words. • Tell me the sentence. Now read it with pauses after each group of words.

Reread for Fluency

Routine **Oral Rereading**

1. **Read** Have students read paragraph 1 of p. 414 orally.

2. **Reread** To achieve optimal fluency, students should reread the text three or four times.

3. **Corrective Feedback** Have students read aloud without you. Provide feedback about their phrasing and encourage them to use punctuation cues to pause after complete thoughts. Listen for use of appropriate phrasing.

Routines Flip Chart

Research and Study Skills

Online Phone Directory

TEACH Ask students where they could find the address or phone number of a person or business they want to contact. Students may say they can look it up in a phone book. Explain that an online phone directory can also be used.

• A phone directory lists names and phone numbers. It may contain residences (white pages), businesses (yellow pages), or both.

• Show students a print directory. Show how the words at the top of the pages can be used to find a phone number.

• Then demonstrate how to find an online directory, using the key words *white pages* or *yellow pages* on a search engine.

• Once in the directory, type in the name of the person or business you want to find, or the category of business—such as *restaurant* or *bicycles.* Include a city or zip code. Provide students with the names of businesses in your community. Have students work in pairs to find the location and phone number of each, using an online phone directory. Have them use text features such as headings to locate information. Make sure students can also use a printed directory.

GUIDE PRACTICE Discuss these questions:

When would you use an online telephone directory? (When you want to call a business but you don't have the number.)

How are online phone directories and phone books alike and different? (Possible response: Both list phone numbers for residences, businesses, or both. An online phone directory is electronic; a phone book is a printed source.)

ON THEIR OWN Have students read and complete pp. 218–219 of the *Reader's and Writer's Notebook.*

⬡STREET INTERACTIVE
www.ReadingStreet.com
Teacher Resources
• Reader's and Writer's Notebook

Reader's and Writer's Notebook, pp. 218–219

ELL

Professional Development: What ELL Experts Say About Oral Reading "Teachers periodically can have students tape-record their oral reading. Ideally, students should be given the option to choose the selection they want to read, to rehearse it, and, when ready, to tape-record their performance.... If the child is bi-literate, the teacher could suggest that the child make tapes in both languages." —Dr. Georgia Earnest García

---

FLUENCY

In Reading Street

Reread for Fluency Students have opportunities to reread the same text orally several times throughout the week. After the teacher models an aspect of fluent reading, students engage in repeated oral reading as the teacher monitors fluency and provides guidance and feedback.

Because Research Says

Perhaps the best known of the strategies designed to support fluency development is that of repeated readings. Generally, the students involved in using this strategy enjoy seeing the gains they make through their tracking of the changes in their reading and experience gratification when making visible improvement over a short period of time. —(Kuhn, 2003)

INFORMATIONAL TEXT

In Reading Street

Research and Study Skills Each week, students learn a specific research, study, or technology skill. Instruction includes a review of terms related to the skill, a practice activity with questions that can be answered by students, and an additional activity that can be used to assess students' understanding. Students then apply the skill to their Research and Inquiry project that week.

Because Research Says

A key to good critical thinking and reading is checking sources of information and verifying ideas. —(McKee and Ogle, 2005)

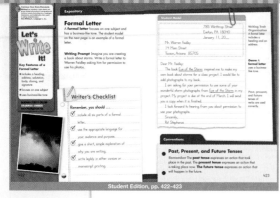

Student Edition, pp. 422–423

Writing (Zoom in)

Formal Letter

Writing Trait: Organization

DISPLAY RUBRIC Display Scoring Rubric 14 from the *Teacher Resources DVD-ROM* and review the criteria for each trait under each score. Then, using the model in the Student Edition, choose students to explain why the model should score a 4 for one of the traits. If a student offers that the model should score below 4 for a particular trait, the student should offer support for that response. Remind students that this is the rubric that will be used to evaluate the formal letter they write.

Scoring Rubric — Formal Letter

	4	3	2	1
Focus/Ideas	Formal letter is clearly focused	Formal letter is generally focused	Formal letter is lacking focus	Formal letter is without focus
Organization	Formal letter is well organized; includes salutation, body, and closing	Formal letter is organized; includes salutation, body, and closing	Formal letter is organized; may be missing one or more of the following: salutation, body, or closing	Formal letter lacks organization; may be missing one or more of the following: salutation, body, or closing
Voice	Informative, engaging voice	Usually informative voice	Voice unsure	No clear voice
Word Choice	Uses a formal tone throughout	Uses mostly a formal tone throughout	Uses some formal, but mostly informal tone	Lacks formal tone; mostly informal
Sentences	Variety of well-constructed sentences	Mostly well-constructed sentences	Few well-constructed sentences	Fragments and run-on sentences
Conventions	Few, if any, errors; verb tenses used correctly	Several minor errors; most verb tenses used are correct	Many errors; many incorrect verb tenses used	Numerous errors; verb tenses used incorrectly

OUTLINE Have students refer to the outlines that they worked on yesterday. If their outlines are not complete, give students additional time to complete their prewriting.

WRITE You will be using your outline as you write the draft of your formal letter. When you are drafting, don't worry if your letter does not sound exactly as you want it to. You will have a chance to revise it tomorrow.

eStreet Interactive
www.ReadingStreet.com

Pearson eText
• Student Edition

Teacher Resources
• Scoring Rubric

Access for All

A Advanced
Provide students with a rich writing sample of a formal letter to analyze formal tone. Have them circle the words that help to create the formal tone.

ELL

Support Drafting Guide students to identify complimentary phrases about Warren Faidley in the model on p. 423. Have students work with partners to create word webs of complimentary expressions that may be useful in their compositions.

Eye of the Storm **423a**

Common Core State Standards
Writing 2a. Introduce a topic clearly and group related information in paragraphs and sections; include formatting (e.g., headings), illustrations, and multimedia when useful to aiding comprehension. **Writing 4.** Produce clear and coherent writing in which the development and organization are appropriate to task, purpose, and audience. **Also Language 1., 3.c.**

Let's Write It!

WRITE A FORMAL LETTER Use pp. 422–423 in the Student Edition. Direct students to read the key features of formal letters, which appear on p. 422. Remind students that they can refer to the information in the Writer's Checklist as they write their own formal letter.

Read the student model on p. 423. Point out the salutation, body, and closing in the model.

CONNECT TO CONVENTIONS Remind students that the tense of a verb tells when an action happens. The present tense tells about action occurring in the present. The past tense tells about action that happened in the past. The future tense tells about future action. Point out the correct use of verb tenses in the model.

WRITING

In Reading Street

Let's Write It! Each week the writing lesson focuses on key features of a genre, provides a close study of a student writing model, and continues through the stages of the writing process.

Because Research Says

Students need to see models of good writing and practice identifying the conventions that make it ready for publication or readable for the intended audience. The model is shared and discussed during the writing process, not in isolation.
—(Anderson, 2007)

WRITING

In Reading Street

Scoring Rubric Rubrics allow teachers to judge students' written work based on the traits of good writing. Students can use the scoring rubric to understand expectations and as a checklist for self-evaluation.

Because Research Says

To know how well students are doing, teachers and administrators should use or consider (1) extended writing samples; (2) writing in multiple genres; (3) valid rubrics; (4) writing over time, across genres and content areas; and (5) student participation in developing assessment.
—(National Writing Project and Nagin, 2003)

SMALL GROUPS

In Reading Street

Access for All: Advanced Daily advanced lessons enhance the skills taught in the core lesson, provide exposure to more challenging reading and vocabulary, and incorporate independent investigative work.

Because Research Says

Many talented readers read early and above grade level. They typically demonstrate enjoyment of reading, are capable of grasping complex ideas, and possess advanced language skills. Differentiated teaching strategies that address the needs of talented readers include curriculum compacting, acceleration, assigning reading material that is above their current grade level, and allowing independent reading choices. —(Kaplan, 1999; Reis and Renzulli, 1989; VanTassel-Baska, 1996)

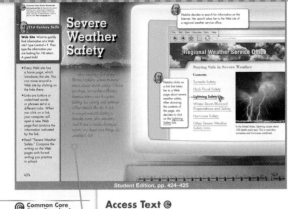

Student Edition, pp. 424–425

Access Text
TEACH 21st Century Skills: Web Sites and Links Have students preview "Severe Weather Safety" on pp. 424–427. Have them look at the structure of the Web site and ask: How can Natalia find information about a specific type of severe weather safety? (skim the contents on the home page and click on a link for the topic she's looking for)

Corrective feedback If... students are unable to explain how to find information on a Web site,
then... use the model to guide students in navigating Web sites and links.

MODEL Natalia's Internet search brings her to the home page for a regional weather service. It lists several links that will take her to other Web pages on the site with information about different topics related to weather safety. The name of each link gives clues to the type of information found on that page. She can skim the list and choose an appropriate topic.

ON THEIR OWN Have students tell what kind of information they would expect to find if they clicked on the *Tornado Safety* link.

Close Reading
SYNTHESIS • TEXT EVIDENCE On pages 424–425, Natalia clicks on the *Lightning Safety* link because thunderstorms occur where she lives in Illinois. Think back to the selection *Eye of the Storm*. Which link on p. 425 might a resident of Miami click on? Why? (In *Eye of the Storm*, we learned that Miami is a place where hurricanes hit. A person who lives there should click on the *Hurricane Safety* link to learn how to stay safe during hurricanes.)

INFERENCE How would predicting and setting a purpose be helpful to Natalia when viewing the Web site and links on pp. 424–425? (This Web site offers a lot of information. It would be helpful for Natalia to set a clear purpose when she begins her search so she doesn't spend time looking at sites that are not useful. Predicting what she might find before clicking on a link will help her locate the answer to her question without following links to unrelated information.)

Common Core State Standards
Informational Text 5. Describe the overall structure (e.g., chronology, comparison, cause/effect, problem/ solution) of events, ideas, concepts, or information in a text or part of a text. Also Language 3.c.

eStreet Interactive
www.ReadingStreet.com
Pearson eText
• Student Edition

Access for All

SI Strategic Intervention
Work with students to identify the different features of a Web site. Help students write down the name of the feature and a short explanation of each.

A Advanced
Have students choose a weather safety topic and locate a Web site where they can find more information about that topic. Then have them write a summary of the information that Web site offers.

ELL
Technology Terms Remind students that the terminology we use to describe Web site features is different from everyday language. Open a Web page on your computer and review the terminology with students, including:
• **tool bar:** the strip at the top of a Web page with preset link buttons that take you to your favorite Web sites
• **links:** other Web sites that are connected to the information on the Web site you are looking at
• **home page:** the introductory page of a Web site

Eye of the Storm **425a**

INFORMATIONAL TEXT

In Reading Street

Science in Reading On Day 4, students read a short companion text to the main selection that is related to the week's concepts. Many of these paired selections are nonfiction texts linked to science and social studies concepts.

Because Research Says

Many young children show a high degree of interest in nonfiction texts, suggesting not only that they can interact successfully with such text but also that they should be given opportunities to do so. Informational text can play a role in building children's knowledge about the world around them, in developing their vocabulary, and in motivating them to read. —(Duke and Tower, 2004)

21ST CENTURY SKILLS

In Reading Street

21st Century Skills Once per unit, the Day 4 paired selection focuses on the skills and strategies students need to write, send, and respond to e-mail; access the Web; use a search engine; or use online directories and reference sources.

Because Research Says

The Internet has entered our classrooms faster than books, television, computers, the telephone, or any other technology for information and communications. Moreover, the Internet will be the vehicle for a host of new technologies that will continue to enter the classroom, regularly requiring new literacies from all of us. One of the more consistent findings from research in this area is that students are highly motivated and interested in these new literacies. —(Leu, 2002)

Student Edition, pp. 428–429

Common Core State Standards

Language 4.b. Use common, grade-appropriate Greek and Latin affixes and roots as clues to the meaning of a word (e.g., telegraph, photograph, autograph). **Also Foundational Skills 4., 4.b., Speaking/Listening 5.**

Fluency

Appropriate Phrasing

GUIDE PRACTICE Use the Fluency activity as an assessment tool. Be sure the passage is at least 200 words long. As students read, make sure they are reading at a natural rate and are pausing after complete thoughts.

Don't Wait Until Friday! MONITOR PROGRESS Check Fluency

FORMATIVE ASSESSMENT As students reread, monitor their progress toward their individual fluency goals.
Current Goal: 105–115 words correct per minute
End-of-Year Goal: 130 words correct per minute

If... students cannot read fluently at a rate of 105–115 words correct per minute, then... have students practice with text at their independent levels.

428–429 Patterns in Nature • Unit 3 • Week 4

Vocabulary Skill

Root Words

TEACH ROOT WORDS • WORD STRUCTURE Write the following sentence on the board: *It was built with thick concrete walls and looked like a fortress.* Tell students that *fortress* comes from a Middle English word that means "strong." Ask students to determine the meaning of *fortress* ("a place that is heavily protected") by using the root *fort*. Encourage them to use the context clues "thick concrete walls" to help them understand the word.

GUIDE PRACTICE Have students use the Old English root *port*, meaning "haven or harbor," to determine the meaning of the word *port*.

ON THEIR OWN Have students determine the meanings of other words that use the root *fort*, meaning "strong." Use the words *forte* ("strong point") and *fort* ("a strong building") as examples. Then have students use those words in sentences.

Media Literacy

Weather Broadcast

TEACH Tell students that people depend upon weather forecasts for accurate information so they can prepare for a storm or a sunny day. On television, a broadcaster forecasts the weather and uses electronic media such as maps, radar images, and other graphics. The director uses design techniques, such as camera close-ups and sound effects, to influence the report.

GUIDE PRACTICE Have students research information for a weather broadcast. Have them include graphic sources that support their broadcast. Remind them when they give their broadcast to speak slowly and clearly and refer to their graphics. Tell students that as an audience they should listen attentively to the speaker. Encourage them to ask relevant questions and make pertinent comments following the broadcast to help the broadcaster improve his or her report.

ON THEIR OWN Have students read about a weather forecast on p. 429 and prepare their report as the broadcaster and director. Have them explain how their design techniques will influence their report. Encourage volunteers to present their broadcast to the class.

STREET INTERACTIVE
www.ReadingStreet.com
Pearson eText
• Student Edition

Weather Broadcast
Remind students that they should speak at a slow and steady rate, enunciate their words, and use appropriate volume to maintain listeners' attention. Remind the audience to listen attentively and to ask relevant questions to clarify understanding of the information.

Bridge to Common Core

PRESENTATION OF KNOWLEDGE/IDEAS
As students present their weather broadcasts, they should adapt their speech to emulate a television meteorologist who is communicating with at-home viewers. They should use appropriate phrasing and present their broadcasts in an organized fashion. Students can make strategic use of digital media and/or visual displays by presenting their weather data on computer or posterboard versions of maps, radar images, bar graphs, and other graphics.

ELL

Formal and Informal English
Discuss with students formal and informal language. Have students distinguish between formal and informal phrases that could be used in a weather broadcast. For example, *It is 95 degrees today* (formal); *It is hot, hot, hot!* (informal). Have students come up with their own informal phrases to describe the weather.

Eye of the Storm 429a

Content Knowledge
Text-Based Comprehension
Review ⊕Cause and Effect
Vocabulary Skill
Review ⊕Root Words
Word Analysis
Review ⊕Latin Roots
Literary Terms
Review ⊕Personification
Assessment
Fluency
Comprehension
Research and Inquiry
Communicate
Spelling
Compound Words
Conventions
Past, Present, and Future Tenses
Writing
Formal Letter

Materials
• Student Edition
• Weekly Test
• Reader's and Writer's Notebook

Bridge to Common Core

INTEGRATION OF KNOWLEDGE/IDEAS
This week, students have integrated content presented in diverse media and analyzed how different texts address similar topics. They have developed knowledge about weather patterns to expand the unit topic of Patterns in Nature.

Social Studies Knowledge Goals
Students have learned that storms
• affect people, animals, and other things
• have different qualities
• require preparation and safety

429f Patterns in Nature • Unit 3 • Week 4

Content Knowledge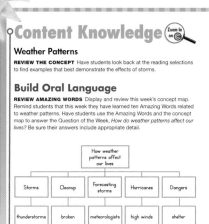

Weather Patterns

REVIEW THE CONCEPT Have students look back at the reading selections to find examples that best demonstrate the effects of storms.

Build Oral Language

REVIEW AMAZING WORDS Display and review this week's concept map. Remind students that this week they have learned ten Amazing Words related to weather patterns. Have students use the Amazing Words and the concept map to answer the Question of the Week, *How do weather patterns affect our lives?* Be sure their answers include appropriate detail.

```
                    How weather
                    patterns affect
                     our lives

  Storms     Cleanup    Forecasting   Hurricanes    Dangers
                          storms

thunderstorms  broken   meteorologists  high winds    shelter

  hurricanes    torn    unpredictable   powerful      ditch

  blizzards   wreckage    estimate      severe       shatter

  tornadoes    littered     maps      unpredictable  destruction
```

Build Oral Vocabulary

Team Talk **CONNECT TO AMAZING IDEAS** Have pairs of students discuss how the Question of the Week connects to the question for this unit of study, *What are some patterns in nature?* Tell students to use the concept map and what they have learned from the week's discussions and reading selections to form an Amazing Idea—a realization or "big idea" about Patterns in Nature. Remind partners to answer questions with appropriate detail and to give suggestions that build on each other's ideas. Then ask pairs to share their Amazing Ideas with the class.

Amazing Ideas might include these key concepts:
• Hurricanes and tornadoes are powerful storms that affect the lives of many people.
• Meteorologists study patterns in nature to predict hurricanes and other storms.
• Everyone should seek shelter to stay safe during severe weather.

WRITE ABOUT IT Have students write a few sentences about their Amazing Idea, beginning with "This week I learned . . ."

It's Friday
MONITOR PROGRESS **Check Oral Vocabulary**

FORMATIVE ASSESSMENT Have individuals use this week's Amazing Words to describe the effects of different storms. Monitor students' abilities to use the Amazing Words and note which words you need to reteach.

If... students have difficulty using the Amazing Words,
then... reteach using the Oral Vocabulary Routine, pp. 403a, 406b, 416b, 424b, OV•4.

⊕STREET INTERACTIVE
www.ReadingStreet.com
Concept Talk Video
Teacher Resources
• Amazing Word Cards
Story Sort

Amazing Words

tornado	hurricane
shelter	severe
ditch	blizzard
unpredictable	meteorologists
powerful	estimate

ELL

Check Concepts and Language Use the Day 5 instruction on ELL Poster 14 to monitor students' understanding of the lesson concept.
Concept Map Work with students to add new words to the concept map.

Eye of the Storm 429g

ORAL LANGUAGE

In Reading Street

Content Knowledge The class revisits the weekly concept and the Question of the Week using the week's concept map. Students apply the information they've learned and the Amazing Words to create Amazing Ideas related to the weekly concept.

Because Research Says

Making word meanings and relationships visible is another way to involve students actively in constructing word meaning. Semantic webs, maps, organizers, or other relational charts not only graphically display attributes of meanings, but also provide a memory organizer for later word use. —(Blachowicz and Fisher, 2002)

Common Core State Standards
Foundational Skills 4. Read with sufficient accuracy and fluency to support comprehension. **Foundational Skills 4.c.** Use context to confirm or self-correct word recognition and understanding, rereading as necessary.

Plan to Assess Fluency
☐ Week 1 Advanced
☐ Week 2 Strategic Intervention
☐ Week 3 On-Level
☑ This week assess Strategic Intervention students.
☐ Week 5 Assess any students you have not yet checked during this unit.

Set individual goals for students to enable them to reach the year-end goal.
• Current Goal: 105–115 WCPM
• Year-End Goal: 130 WCPM

Assessment

Monitor Progress

FLUENCY Make two copies of the fluency passage on page 429k. As the student reads the text aloud, mark mistakes on your copy. Also mark where the student is at the end of one minute. To check the student's comprehension of the passage, have him or her retell what was read. To figure words correct per minute (WCPM), subtract the number of mistakes from the total number of words read in one minute.

RATE

| Corrective feedback | If... students cannot read fluently at a rate of 105–115 WCPM, then... make sure they practice with text at their independent reading level. Provide additional fluency practice by pairing nonfluent readers with fluent readers. |
| | If... students already read at 140 WCPM, then... have them read a book of their choice independently. |

Day 5 **SMALL GROUP TIME • Differentiate Reteaching, p. SG•49**

OL On-Level	SI Strategic Intervention	A Advanced
• **Practice** Subjects and Predicates	• **Review** Subjects and Predicates	• **Extend** Subjects and Predicates
• **Reread** *Reading Street Sleuth,* pp. 38–39	• **Reread** *Reading Street Sleuth,* pp. 38–39	• **Reread** *Reading Street Sleuth,* pp. 38–39
		• **Communicate** Inquiry Project

Name _____

After Katrina: Making Things Better

When Hurricane Katrina hit New Orleans in 2005, most folks — 10
thought their city was ready. Their homes were strong. They had built — 22
flood walls. Levees made the banks of the nearby lakes strong, so they — 35
would not flood the city. People thought their city was safe. — 46

They were wrong, though. Huge numbers of homes were destroyed — 56
in the strong winds. The levees failed in over fifty places. The flood — 69
walls did not hold. After the storm hit, over 80 percent of the city was — 84
under water. In some places there was 20 feet of water! — 95

Since then, New Orleans has been slowly rebuilding. The — 104
government and the people are working with each other. Engineers — 114
have figured out what went wrong. They have worked to find ways to — 127
make things better and stronger. As they rebuild homes, they are using — 139
better designs and stronger construction. The roofs and walls will be — 150
able to stand up to higher winds. To protect the city, engineers have — 163
built stronger flood walls. They have come up with new and better — 175
ways to build the levees. This time they will stand up to heavier flood — 189
waters. — 190

Nobody knows when and if another storm will hit. The people — 201
of New Orleans, though, are working so that next time they will — 213
be ready. — 215

MONITOR PROGRESS
• Check Fluency

Eye of the Storm **429k**

FORMATIVE ASSESSMENT

In Reading Street

Assessment On Day 5, teachers administer assessments. To assess fluency, the teacher takes a timed sample of students' oral reading from reproducible pages. A written assessment monitors progress in the week's target comprehension skill.

Because Research Says

Providing ongoing assessment of student reading progress may be one of the most valuable things teachers can do. The most valuable way to monitor student progress in fluency is to take timed measures of the number of words they read correctly in one minute.
—(Vaughn and Linan-Thompson, 2004)

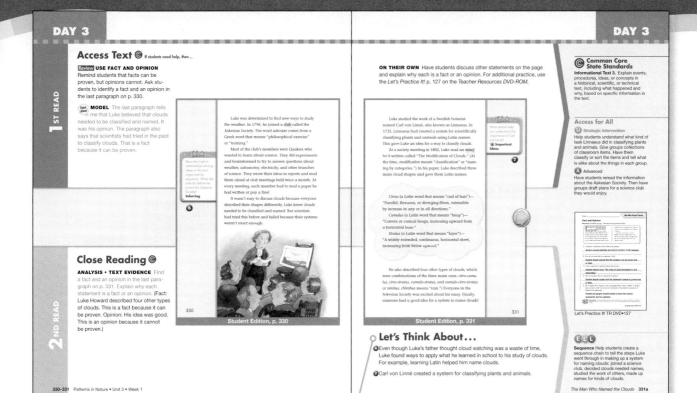

In Reading Street

Let's Think About The first main selection of every unit, all of the paired selections (except 21st Century Skills lessons), and the first spread of each unit's Poetry Collection are annotated with thought-provoking Let's Think About questions. Main selection questions allow students to access the text by providing practice with the target skills and strategies. Paired selection questions guide students in identifying the elements of genre. Poetry Collection questions allow students to fully appreciate the poems by identifying the elements of poetry. All of these questions guide students in becoming strategic readers.

Because Research Says

True comprehension goes beyond literal understanding and involves the reader's interaction with text. If students are to become thoughtful, insightful readers, they must merge their thinking with the text and extend their thinking beyond a superficial understanding. —(Harvey and Goudvis, 2007)

ⒼCommon Core State Standards

Informational Text 5. Describe the overall structure (e.g., chronology, comparison, cause/effect, problem/ solution) of events, ideas, concepts, or information in a text or part of a text. **Foundational Skills 4.** Read with sufficient accuracy and fluency to support comprehension. **Language 6.** Acquire and use accurately grade-appropriate general academic and domain specific words and phrases, including those that signal precise actions, emotions, or states of being (e.g., *quizzed, whined, stammered*) and that are basic to a particular topic (e.g., *wildlife, conservation,* and *endangered* when discussing animal preservation). **Also Informational Text 3.**

Independent Reading Options

Trade Book Library

ⒸSTREET INTERACTIVE
www.ReadingStreet.com
Teacher Guides are available on the Leveled Reader Database.

ⒺⓁⓁ
If... students need more scaffolding and practice with **Vocabulary**, then... use the activities on pp. DI•92–DI•93 in the Teacher Resources section on SuccessNet.

SG•50 Patterns in Nature • Unit 3 • Week 4

OL On-Level

① Build Word Knowledge
Practice Amazing Words

DEFINE IT Elicit the definition for the word *tornado* from students. Ask: How would you describe a *tornado* to another student? (Possible response: A *tornado* is a twisting funnel of air.) Clarify or give a definition when necessary. Continue with the words *shelter* and *ditch*.

Team Talk **TALK ABOUT IT** Have students internalize meanings. Ask: How can you pair the Amazing Words together in a sentence? (Possible response: If you are outside during a *tornado*, take *shelter* in a *ditch*.) Allow time for students to play with the words. Review the concept map with students. Discuss other words they can add to the concept map.

② Text-Based Comprehension
Read

READ ALOUD "Tornado Sirens—What's the Use?" Have partners read "Tornado Sirens—What's the Use?" from *Reading Street Sleuth* on pp. 38–39. Discuss the concept words *siren, obsolete,* and *panic.* Then have partners reread the selection.

ACCESS TEXT Response to Reading

1. How is a cell phone different from a tornado siren when it comes to tornado warnings? (Cell phones can tell you where the storm is headed, locate the nearest tornado shelter, and tell you when you are in danger. Tornado sirens are more general and can't tell you when you are in danger.)

2. Find and describe a cause-and-effect relationship from the text. (Cause: The tornado siren sounded. Effect: The out-of-town visitor panicked.) Encourage students to find additional causes and effects.

3. **Performance Task** Have partners return to the text to find reasons the author gives to support the argument that tornado sirens are obsolete and to determine whether the reasons are valid. Students can use a T-chart, listing reasons in one column and whether the reason is valid in the other. Students can work on this during independent time on Days 2, 3, and 4.

OL On-Level

① Build Word Knowledge
Practice Selection Vocabulary

DEFINE IT Discuss the definition for the word *shatter* with students. Ask: How would you describe *shatter* to another student? (Possible response: *Shatter* is to break into a million pieces.) Continue with the remaining words.

| destruction | expected | forecasts |
| inland | shatter | surge |

Team Talk **TALK ABOUT IT** Have pairs use the selection vocabulary in sentences to internalize meaning. Ask: How can you pair the selection vocabulary words together in a sentence? (Possible response: No one *forecasted* the extent of the *destruction* from the *hurricane*.) Allow time for students to play with the words and then share their sentences.

② Read
Eye of the Storm

If you read *Eye of the Storm* during whole group time, then use the following instruction.

ACCESS TEXT Reread the top paragraphs on pp. 410 and 411. Ask questions to check understanding. What is Warren Faidley's job? (He photographs storms.) How do weather patterns affect where Warren goes at different times of the year? (Warren travels to find tornadoes in the spring, thunderstorms in the summer, and hurricanes in the fall. He stays home and sells his photographs when there are no storms.)

Have students identify sections from today's reading that they did not completely understand. Reread them aloud and clarify misunderstandings.

If you are reading *Eye of the Storm* during small group time, then return to pp. 408–415a to guide the reading.

ⒸSTREET INTERACTIVE
Pearson eText
• Student Edition
• Leveled Reader Database
• Reading Street Sleuth

More Reading for Group Time

Severe Weather: **Storms**

ON-LEVEL

Reviews
• Cause and Effect
• Predict and Set Purpose
• Selection Vocabulary

Use this suggested Leveled Reader or other text at student's instructional level.

ⒸSTREET INTERACTIVE
www.ReadingStreet.com
Use the Leveled Reader Database for lesson plans and student pages for *Severe Weather: Storms.*

Eye of the Storm SG•51

······ SMALL GROUPS ······

In Reading Street

On-Level Instruction Daily Small Group Time lessons focus on appropriate instructional strategies for students reading at grade level.

Because Research Says

Smaller group ratios increase the likelihood of academic success through student-teacher interactions, individualization of instruction, student on-task behavior, and teacher monitoring of student progress and feedback. —(Vaughn, et al., 2003)

······ SMALL GROUPS ······

In Reading Street

Reading Street Sleuth A core component of small group instruction is *Reading Street Sleuth.* Students at all ability levels read the same weekly selection. The accompanying instruction provides the scaffolding necessary for all students to access challenging texts and become thoughtful, inquisitive learners.

Because Research Says

. . . comprehension is not simple, nor does it develop overnight in terms of clues to aid understanding. Little is given to the reader outside the text. For that reason, readers must engage in an active construction of meaning, in which they grapple with the text and apply their earlier knowledge as they question, analyze, and probe. In the process, they learn to build knowledge and go beyond the wisdom of the author to think their own thoughts. —(Wolf and Barzillai, 2009)

SI Strategic Intervention

SI Strategic Intervention

⊚**STREET INTERACTIVE**
www.ReadingStreet.com
Pearson eText
• Student Edition

SMALL GROUP TIME

Ⓒ Common Core State Standards

Informational Text 3. Explain events, procedures, ideas, or concepts in a historical, scientific, or technical text, including what happened and why, based on specific information in the text. **Language 6.** Acquire and use accurately grade-appropriate general academic and domain specific words and phrases, including those that signal precise actions, emotions, or states of being (e.g., *quizzed, whined, stammered*) and that are basic to a particular topic (e.g., *wildlife, conservation, and endangered* when discussing animal preservation). **Also Informational Text 5.**

① Build Word Knowledge

Reteach Selection Vocabulary

DEFINE IT Describe *destruction* to a friend. Give a definition when necessary. Restate the word in student-friendly terms and clarify meaning with a visual. *Destruction* means great damage, such as is caused by a hurricane. Page 419 shows destruction from a hurricane.

| destruction | expected | forecasts |
| inland | shatter | surge |

Team Talk **TALK ABOUT IT** Have you seen destruction? Turn and talk to your partner about this. Allow time for students to discuss. Ask for examples. Rephrase students' examples for usage when necessary or to correct misunderstandings. Continue with the remaining words.

> **Corrective feedback** **If...** students need more practice with selection vocabulary, **then...** use the *Envision It! Pictured Vocabulary Cards.*

② Read

Eye of the Storm

If you read *Eye of the Storm* during whole group time, then use the instruction below.

ACCESS TEXT Reread the top paragraphs on pp. 410 and 411. Ask questions to check understanding. Who is Warren Faidley? (a storm chaser) What does he do? (takes photographs of storms) What three types of storms does he photograph? (tornadoes, thunderstorms, hurricanes) When does he photograph each type of storm? (tornadoes in the spring, thunderstorms in the summer, hurricanes in the late summer and fall)

Have students identify sections they did not understand. Reread them aloud. Clarify the meaning of each section to build understanding.

If you are reading *Eye of the Storm* during small group time, then return to pp. 408–415a to guide the reading.

Independent Reading Options

Trade Book Library

⊚**STREET INTERACTIVE**
www.ReadingStreet.com
Teacher Guides are available on the Leveled Reader Database.

SG•56   Patterns in Nature • Unit 3 • Week 4

① Build Word Knowledge

Develop Vocabulary

REREAD FOR VOCABULARY Reread the first paragraph of *Eye of the Storm*, p. 416. Let's read this paragraph to find out what the word *anemometer* means. (An *anemometer* is an instrument for measuring the force and speed of wind.) To help students understand the word *anemometer*, ask questions related to the context: What are Steve and Warren doing? What is an instrument? How fast was the wind going?

> **Corrective feedback** **If...** students have difficulty understanding the word *anemometer*, **then...** guide students to use online sources to find more information.

② Read

Eye of the Storm

If you read *Eye of the Storm* during whole group time, then use the instruction below.

CLOSE READING Read pp. 416–417. Have students search through the text to find time references that help the reader organize the events of the story. Make a list of these words and phrases in the order they occur and then retell what happened in the story. *(During the next hour; When; Around 3:45; As; Later; About 5:15; Now)*

Now use the times you listed to retell what happened in this part of the story. (Steve and Warren tried to measure wind speed. They stopped when the wind increased to 65 mph. Around 3:45 in the morning the winds became stronger and blew in windows. As the glass broke, car alarms went off. Later the winds became even stronger. About 5:15 the winds reached their peak. The winds got so loud it sounded like jet engines.)

If you are reading *Eye of the Storm* during small group time, then return to pp. 416–419a to guide the reading.

ⒺⓁⓁ **If...** students need more scaffolding and practice with the **Main Selection**, **then...** use the activities on p. DI•97 in the Teacher Resources section on SuccessNet.

Eye of the Storm   SG•57

········ SMALL GROUPS ········

In Reading Street

Strategic Intervention

Instruction Daily Small Group Time lessons provide struggling readers with more intensive instruction, more scaffolding, more practice with critical skills, and more opportunities to respond.

Because Research Says

A combination of explicit and systematic instruction with carefully scaffolded instruction that provides modeling and feedback is associated with improved academic outcomes for students with reading and learning disabilities. —(Vaughn and Linan-Thompson, 2003)

········ SMALL GROUPS ········

In Reading Street

Reteach During Small Group Time, struggling readers receive more explicit, intensive instruction focused on critical elements of reading, such as vocabulary and comprehension.

Because Research Says

Students who struggle with reading may require 10 times as many practice opportunities as their peers. When a student is one of four in a group, he or she has five times the opportunity to respond with specific feedback than a student in a group of 20. In homogeneous small groups, teachers can more easily provide immediate, explicit feedback to students, making it less likely that errors will become internalized and be repeated. —(Swanson and Vaughn, 2011)

Research into Practice   **87**

Common Core State Standards

Informational Text 5. Describe the overall structure (e.g., chronology, comparison, cause/effect, problem/solution) of events, ideas, concepts, or information in a text or part of a text. **Informational Text 7.** Interpret information presented visually, orally, or quantitatively (e.g., in charts, graphs, diagrams, time lines, animations, or interactive elements on Web pages) and explain how the information contributes to an understanding of the text in which it appears. **Also Writing 10., Speaking/Listening 1.c.**

1 Build Word Knowledge

Develop Vocabulary

REREAD FOR VOCABULARY Reread the first paragraph on p. 416. Let's read this paragraph to find out what *anemometer* means. (An *anemometer* is an instrument for measuring wind speed and force.) Discuss meaning and context with students.

2 Read

Eye of the Storm

If you read *Eye of the Storm* during whole group time, then use the instruction below.

CLOSE READING Read pp. 416–417. Have students create a T-chart with the heads **Imagery** and **Structure**. Have students search through the text to find references to different sounds. Have them record the sound descriptions (under **Imagery**) in the order in which they occur, and then find words that help structure the scene (under **Structure**).

Imagery	Structure
• carrying raindrops sideways,	• During the next hour,
• bursts of breaking glass.	• When

Ask: What idea is the author developing? (The sounds change as winds get stronger until the storm peaks and the winds drown out the other sounds.) Why does the author appeal to the sense of sound? (The text says they can't see anything in the darkness, so they describe what they hear.)

If you are reading *Eye of the Storm* during small group time, then return to pp. 416–419a to guide the reading.

3 Inquiry: Extend Concepts

INVESTIGATE Provide time for students to investigate their topics in books or online. If necessary, help them locate information that is focused on their topics.

Independent Reading Options

Trade Book Library

@STREET INTERACTIVE
www.ReadingStreet.com
Teacher Guides are available on the Leveled Reader Database.

ELL

If... students need more scaffolding and practice with the **Main Selection**, then... use the activities on p. DI•97 in the Teacher Resources section on SuccessNet.

SG•62 Patterns in Nature • Unit 3 • Week 4

---

1 Build Word Knowledge

Extend Amazing Words and Selection Vocabulary

tornado	powerful	blizzard
shelter	hurricane	meteorologists
ditch	severe	estimate
unpredictable		

destruction	expected	forecasts
inland	shatter	surge

Team Talk Have students practice building complex sentences. Display a sentence starter and have students add oral phrases or clauses using the Amazing Words and the selection vocabulary. The powerful hurricane _____. (The *powerful* hurricane was so *severe* / that there was much *destruction inland* / and many windows were *shattered*.) Guide students to add at least three phrases or clauses per sentence.

2 Read

"Severe Weather Safety"

BEFORE READING Have students read the information about Web sites on pp. 424–427. How is the text structure different from *Eye of the Storm?* ("Severe Weather Safety" uses bold words, underlined words, explanatory boxes, and lists.)

DURING READING Have students discuss "Severe Weather Safety" with a partner. What search words could you use to research severe weather safety? (storms, weather, tornadoes, hurricanes, safety)

AFTER READING Meet with students to discuss the article before they do the Get Online! activity.

3 Inquiry: Extend Concepts

ORGANIZE INFORMATION Provide time for students to organize their information into a format that will effectively communicate their findings to their audience. Provide any necessary materials.

@STREET INTERACTIVE
www.ReadingStreet.com
Pearson eText
• Student Edition

Independent Reading Options

Trade Book Library

@STREET INTERACTIVE
www.ReadingStreet.com
Teacher Guides are available on the Leveled Reader Database.

Eye of the Storm SG•63

SMALL GROUP TIME

········ SMALL GROUPS ········

In Reading Street

Advanced Instruction Daily Small Group Time lessons for students reading above grade level enhance the skills taught in the core lesson, provide exposure to more challenging reading and vocabulary, and incorporate independent investigative work. Activities provide advanced readers additional opportunities to engage in critical and creative thinking, and to focus on problem-solving skills.

Because Research Says

In general, grouping academically talented students together for instruction has been found to produce positive achievement outcomes when the curriculum provided to students in different groups is appropriately differentiated. In other words, it is the instruction that occurs within groups that makes grouping an appropriate instructional strategy. —(Reis, et al., 2003)

········ SMALL GROUPS ········

In Reading Street

Extending Concepts Through Inquiry Daily activities allow advanced readers to respond to reading selections and extend concepts through creative thinking, critical thinking, problem solving, and independent investigative work.

Because Research Says

Classroom teachers can challenge talented readers with higher-level questioning that extends with the depth of students' contact with good literature. Rich, complex reading provides the possibility of multiple interpretations of literature that can challenge students at all levels. —(Reis, et al., 2003)

Research Bibliography

Anderson, Jeff. *Mechanically Inclined: Building Grammar, Usage, and Style into Writer's Workshop.* Stenhouse Publishers, 2005.

Anderson, R., E. Hiebert, J. Scott, and I. Wilkinson. "The Report of the Commission on Reading." *Becoming a Nation of Readers.* The National Institute of Education, 1985.

Armbruster, B. B., F. Lehr and J. Osborn. *Put Reading First: The Research Building Blocks for Teaching Children to Read.* Partnership for Reading, 2001.

Beck, Isabel L., Margaret G. McKeown, Rebecca L. Hamilton, and Linda Kucan. *Bringing Words to Life: Robust Vocabulary Instruction.* The Guilford Press, 2002.

Blachowicz, Camille and Peter J. Fisher. *Teaching Vocabulary in All Classrooms,* 2nd ed. Merrill Prentice Hall, 2002.

Block, Cathy Collins and Michael Pressley. "Best Practices in Comprehension Instruction." *Best Practices in Literary Instruction.* The Guilford Press, 2003.

Coyne, Michael D., Deborah C. Simmons, and Edward J. Kame'enui. "Vocabulary Instruction for Young Children at Risk of Experiencing Reading Difficulties." *Vocabulary Instruction: Research to Practice.* The Guilford Press, 2004.

Cummins, Jim. "The Three Pillars of English Language Learning." *Pearson Scott Foresman EL Handbook Teacher's Manual,* 2010.

Duke, Nell K. and P. David Pearson. "Effective Practices for Developing Reading Comprehension." *What Research Has to Say About Reading Instruction,* 3rd ed. International Reading Association, 2002.

Duke, Nell K., V. Susan Bennett-Armistead, Ebony M. Roberts. "Bridging the Gap Between Learning to Read and Reading to Learn." *Literacy and Young Children: Research-Based Practices.* The Guilford Press, 2003.

Duke, Nell K., P. David Pearson, Stephanie L. Strachan, and Alison K. Billman. "Essential Elements of Fostering and Teaching Reading Comprehension." *What Research Has to Say About Reading Instruction,* 4th ed. International Reading Association, 2011.

Ehri, Linnea C. and Simone R. Nunes. "The Role of Phonemic Awareness in Learning to Read." *What Research Has to Say About Reading Instruction,* 3rd ed. International Reading Association, 2002.

Ehri, Linnea C. "Grapheme-Phoneme Knowledge Is Essential for Learning to Read Words in English." *Word Recognition in Beginning Literacy.* Lawrence Erlbaum Associates, 1992.

Foorman, B. R., and J. Torgesen. "Critical Elements of Classroom and Small-Group Instruction Promote Reading Success in All Children." *Learning Disabilities Research and Practice,* vol. 16, November 2001.

Galda, Lee, and Richard Beach. "Response to Literature as a Cultural Activity." *Theoretical Models and Processes of Reading,* 5th ed. International Reading Association, 2004.

García, Georgia Earnest. "English Learners and Literacy: Best Practices." *Pearson Scott Foresman EL Handbook Teacher's Manual,* 2010.

Gaskins, Irene W. "A Multidimensional Approach to Beginning Literacy." *Literacy and Young Children: Research-Based Practices.* The Guilford Press, 2003.

Ivey, Gay. "Building Comprehension When They're Still Learning to Read the Words." *Comprehension Instruction: Research-Based Best Practices.* The Guilford Press, 2002.

Juel, Connie. "Impact of Early School Experiences," *Handbook of Early Literacy Research,* 2nd ed. The Guilford Press, 2005.

Kaplan, S. "Reading Strategies for Gifted Readers." *Teaching for High Potential,* vol. 1, no. 2, 1999.

Kuhn, M. R., and S. A. Stahl. "Fluency: A Review of Developmental and Remedial Practices." *Journal of Educational Psychology,* vol. 95, 2003.

Kuhn, Melanie. "How Can I Help Them Pull It All Together? A Guide to Fluent Reading Instruction." *Literacy and Young Children: Research-Based Practices.* The Guilford Press, 2003.

Krashen, Stephen D., and Tracy D. Terrell. *The Natural Approach: Language Acquisition in the Classroom.* Alemany Press, 1983.

Leu, D. J. Jr., C. K. Kinzer, J. Coiro, and D. Cammack. "Toward a Theory of New Literacies Emerging from the Internet and Other Information and Communication Technologies." *Theoretical Models and Processes of Reading,* 5th ed. International Reading Association, 2004.

Leu, Donald and Charles Kinzer. "The Convergence of Literary Instruction with Networked Technologies for Information and Communication." *Reading Research Quarterly,* vol. 35, no. 1, January/February/March 2000.

Leu, Donald. "The New Literacies: Research on Reading Instruction with the Internet." *What Research Has to Say About Reading Instruction,* 3rd ed., International Reading Association, 2002.

McKee, Judith and Donna Ogle. *Integrating Instruction, Literacy and Science.* The Guilford Press, 2005.

Morrow, Lesley Mandel and Linda Gambrell. "Literature-Based Instruction in the Early Years." *Handbook of Early Literacy Research.* The Guilford Press, 2002.

Morrow, L. M., "Story Retelling: A Discussion Strategy to Develop and Assess Comprehension." *Lively Discussions! Fostering Engaged Reading.* International Reading Association, 1996.

National Reading Panel. *Teaching Children to Read.* National Institute of Child Health and Human Development. 1999.

National Writing Project and Carl Nagin. *Because Writing Matters.* Jossey-Bass, 2003.

Noguchi, Rei R. *The English Record.* Winter, 2002.

Ogle, D. and C. L. Blachowicz. "Beyond Literature Circles: Helping Students Comprehend Informational Texts." *Comprehension Instruction: Research-Based Best Practices.* The Guilford Press, 2002.

Paratore, Jeanne and Rachel McCormack. *Teaching Literacy in Second Grade.* The Guilford Press, 2005.

Pearson, P. D., L. R. Roehler, J. A. Dole, and G. G. Duffy. "Developing Expertise in Reading Comprehension." *What Research Says About Reading Instruction,* 2nd ed. International Reading Association, 1992.

Pearson, P. David and Nell K. Duke. "Comprehension Instruction in the Primary Grades." *Comprehension Instruction: Research-Based Best Practices.* The Guilford Press, 2002.

Pressley, M., and C. C. Block. "Summing Up: What Comprehension Instruction Could Be." *Comprehension Instruction: Research-Based Best Practices.* The Guilford Press, 2002.

Pressley, M. "Metacognition and Self-Regulated Comprehension." *What Research Has to Say About Reading Instruction,* 3rd ed. International Reading Association, 2002.

Reis, Sally M., E. Jean Gubbins, Christine Briggs, Fredric J. Schreiber, Susannah Richards, Joan Jacobs, Rebecca D. Eckert, Joseph S. Renzulli, and Margaret Alexander. *Reading Instruction for Talented Readers: Case Studies Documenting Few Opportunities for Continuous Progress* (RM03184). The National Research Center on the Gifted and Talented, University of Connecticut, 2003.

Reis, Sally M., and Joseph S. Renzulli. "Developing Challenging Programs for Gifted Readers." *The Reading Instruction Journal,* vol. 32, 1989.

Samuels, S. J. "Reading Fluency: Its Development and Assessment." *What Research Has to Say About Reading Instruction,* 3rd ed. International Reading Association, 2002.

Seefeldt, Carol and Barbara A. Wasik. *Early Education: Three-, Four-, and Five-Year Olds Go to School,* 2nd ed. Pearson Merrill Prentice Hall, 2006.

Smith, Sylvia B., Deborah C. Simmons, and Edward J. Kame'enui. "Phonological Awareness: Instructional and Curricular Basics and Implications." *What Reading Research Tells Us About Children With Diverse Learning Needs: Bases and Basics.* Lawrence Erlbaum Associates, 1998.

Snow, Catherine E., M. Susan Burns, and Peg Griffin, eds. *Preventing Reading Difficulties in Young Children.* National Research Council, 1998.

Spandel, Vicki. "Assessing With Heart." National Staff Development Council, vol. 27, no. 3, Summer 2006.

_____. *Creating Writers Through 6-Trait Writing Assessment and Instruction,* 2nd ed. Merrill Prentice Hall, 2002.

_____. *Creating Writers Through 6-Trait Writing Assessment and Instruction,* 3rd ed. Addison Wesley Longman, 2001.

_____. *Creating Writers Through 6-Trait Writing Assessment and Instruction,* 4th ed. Allyn and Bacon, 2004.

Stahl, Steven A. and Katherine A. Dougherty Stahl. "Word Wizards All! Teaching Word Meanings in Preschool and Primary Education." *Vocabulary Instruction: Research to Practice.* The Guilford Press, 2004.

Swanson, Elizabeth and Sharon Vaughn. "Implementing a Response to Intervention Model to Improve Reading Outcomes for all Students." *What Research Has to Say About Reading Instruction,* 4th ed. International Reading Association, 2011.

Tatum, Alfred. *Teaching Reading to Black Adolescent Males.* Stenhouse Publishers, 2005.

Taylor, Barbara M., P. David Pearson, Debra S. Peterson, and Michael C. Rodriguez. "The CIERA School Change Framework: An Evidence-Based Approach to Professional Development and School Reading Improvement." *Reading Research Quarterly,* vol. 40, no. 1, January/February/March 2005.

VanTassel-Baska, J. "Effective Curriculum and Instructional Models for Talented Students." *Gifted Child Quarterly,* vol. 30, 1996.

Vaughn, Sharon and Sylvia Linan-Thompson. *Research-Based Methods of Reading Instruction.* Association for Supervision and Curriculum Development, 2004.

_____. "Group Size and Time Allotted to Intervention: Effects for Students with Reading Difficulties." *Preventing and Remediating Reading Difficulties: Bringing Science to Scale.* Baltimore York Press, 2003.

Vaughn, Sharon, Sylvia Linan-Thompson, Kamiar Kouzekanani, Diane Pedrotty, Shirley Dickson, and Shelly Blozis. "Reading Instruction Grouping for Students with Reading Difficulties." *Remedial and Special Education,* vol. 24, no. 5, September/October 2003.

Weaver, Constance. *Grammar for Teachers: Perspectives and Definitions.* NCTE, 1979.

Wiggins, Grant and Jay McTighe. *Understanding by Design.* Pearson Education, Inc., 2006.

Wilkinson, L. C. and E. R. Silliman. "Classroom Language and Literacy Learning." *Handbook of Reading Research,* vol. III. Lawrence Erlbaum Associates, 2000.

Wolf, Maryanne and Mirit Barzillai. "The Importance of Deep Reading." *Educational Leadership.* vol. 66, no. 6, March 2009.

Wong Fillmore, Lily and Catherine E. Snow. "What Teachers Need to Know About Language." *What Teachers Need to Know About Language.* The Center for Applied Linguistics and Delta Systems Co., Inc., 2002.

Wong Fillmore, Lily. "Preparing English Language Learners for Assessment." *Pearson Scott Foresman EL Handbook Teacher's Manual,* 2010.

Wray, David and Maureen Lewis. "But Bonsai Trees Don't Grow in Baskets: Young Children's Talk During Authentic Inquiry." *Lively Discussions! Fostering Engaged Reading.* International Reading Association, 1996.

Zevenenbergen, Andrea and Grover Whitehurst. *On Reading Books to Children: Parents and Teacher.* Lawrence Erlbaum Associates, 2003.